DESEGREGATION

Other books in the
Interpreting Primary Documents series:

Colonial America
Westward Expansion

DESEGREGATION

INTERPRETING PRIMARY DOCUMENTS

Nick Treanor, Book Editor

Daniel Leone, President
Bonnie Szumski, Publisher
Scott Barbour, Managing Editor

GREENHAVEN
PRESS®

THOMSON
————*————™
GALE

San Diego • Detroit • New York • San Francisco • Cleveland
New Haven, Conn. • Waterville, Maine • London • Munich

THOMSON

GALE

LIBRARY OF CONGRESS CATALOGING-IN-PUBLICATION DATA

Desegregation / Nick Treanor, book editor.
        p. cm. — (Interpreting primary documents)
    Includes bibliographical references and index.
    ISBN 0-7377-1302-X (lib. bdg. : alk. paper) —
    ISBN 0-7377-1303-8 (pbk. : alk. paper)
        1. African Americans—Civil rights—History—20th century—Sources. 2. African Americans—Segregation—History—20th century—Sources. 3. School integration—United States—History—20th century—Sources. 4. United States—Race relations—Sources. I. Treanor, Nick. II. Series.
    E185.61 .D47 2003
    305.8'00973—dc21   2002023169

Printed in the United States of America

CONTENTS

Foreword   10

Introduction: Racial Segregation in the United States   12

Chapter 1: The Winds of Change

Chapter Preface   32

1. **The Time for Change Is Now**   34
   by the President's Committee on Civil Rights
   Racial discrimination is widespread in America. It is
   suspect on moral grounds, costly on economic
   grounds, and unwise on foreign policy grounds.

2. **Segregation Is Wrong Because It Harms Blacks**   44
   by Benjamin E. Mays
   Segregation is morally wrong and offends the dignity of black Americans. Blacks want integration not
   because they desire to mix with whites but because
   they want access to the basic services they deserve as
   citizens.

3. **Schools Should Be Segregated**   53
   by James Jackson Kilpatrick
   The case for integration is based on a central mistake. The white race is, as a whole, superior, and
   this justifies school segregation.

4. **Change in the South Is Inevitable**   61
   by Lenoir Chambers
   The Supreme Court judgment in *Brown v. Board of
   Education* was legitimate and unequivocal. White
   Southerners have to accept the ruling and move on.

Chapter 2: The Role of Government

Chapter Preface   68

1. The Supreme Court Judgment Violates the
   Constitution   70
   by Walter F. George et al.
   The U.S. Constitution guarantees states the right to
   determine education policy. The *Brown v. Board of
   Education* ruling violates this guarantee and deserves to be resisted.

2. States Have a Right to Preserve Segregation   75
   by George C. Wallace
   The federal government infringes on the liberty of
   the citizens of Alabama when it imposes desegregation. Races should live apart, and the battle to preserve segregation is divinely inspired.

3. States Should Stay Out of Local Integration
   Efforts   81
   by the Arkansas Gazette
   The issue at hand is no longer about integration but
   about whether state officials are willing to ignore
   the decisions of U.S. courts. By doing so, they interfere with local efforts to comply with such decisions.

4. Citizens Must Obey the Laws   84
   by Dwight D. Eisenhower
   When state and local authorities fail to enforce federal law, the federal government must do so. Whatever one's views on segregation, one should demand
   that federal law be enforced.

5. The Federal Government Does Not Fight for
   Desegregation   90
   by Howard Zinn
   The federal government has a reputation as an ally
   of the civil rights movement. It is actually more interested in preserving its vision of "law and order"
   than it is in defending civil rights.

6. Segregation Is Morally Wrong and Must End   100
by John F. Kennedy
Segregation is a moral outrage, and the federal government must work to end it. Citizens and Congress ought to unite behind new laws against segregation.

Chapter 3: The Place of Protest

Chapter Preface   108

1. The Way to Justice Is Nonviolent Resistance   111
by Martin Luther King Jr.
Those who are oppressed must oppose oppression, but they cannot do so with violence. Nonviolent protest is the right means by which to achieve justice.

2. The Nonviolent Movement   119
by Diane Nash
The struggle against southern racism is a struggle to create a community in which the God-given worth of every human being is recognized and respected. The nonviolent movement is thus applied religion.

3. The Popular Movement Is a Revolt Against the Black Leadership Class   127
by Louis E. Lomax
What is remarkable about the desegregation movement is that it is the work of ordinary blacks, especially young ones. As such, it rejects the view that ordinary blacks need to depend on a leadership class that speaks for them.

4. A Letter from Jail   135
by Patricia Stephens
When the mayor ordered our arrest, we were peacefully protesting racial segregation. I do not mind serving time in jail, however, to promote equality and justice.

5. Do Nonviolent Protesters Try to Provoke
   Violence?   141
   by Jan Howard
   Although the so-called nonviolent movement professes to reject violence, it often relies on white violence to achieve its goals. When such violence fails
   to occur, those involved feel their efforts have been
   futile.

6. The Perspective of the Ordinary White   150
   by Robert Coles
   Some whites in the South were not very active in either promoting or resisting segregation. They saw
   themselves as part of a complex social order over
   which they had little control and for which they
   were not responsible.

Chapter 4: Desegregation in the North
Chapter Preface   160

1. Segregation Exists in the North, Too   163
   by James Peck
   There is racism and segregation in the North, too.
   Many whites do not want blacks to live in their
   neighborhoods.

2. Integration May Not Be the Answer   168
   by James Farmer
   Full integration may not best serve the black cause.
   Rather than assimilating into white communities
   and adopting white lifestyles, blacks ought to cherish and develop their own culture.

3. Racial Equality Is More Important than Racial
   Integration   179
   by the New Republic
   Court-ordered busing is unwise because it disrupts
   communities and ultimately promotes a decline in
   the quality of public education. Quality education is
   more important than integration.

4. Racial Violence in the North   184
by Time

Although Boston is thought to be an enlightened
northern city, racial violence broke out over court-
ordered busing. The problems traditionally thought
to exist only in the South exist in the North as well.

Chronology   189

For Further Research   196

Index   200

FOREWORD

In a debate on the nature of the historian's task, the Canadian intellectual Michael Ignatieff wrote, "I don't think history is a lesson in patriotism. It should be a lesson in truth. And the truth is both painful and many-sided." Part of Ignatieff's point was that those who seek to understand the past should guard against letting prejudice or patriotism interfere with the truth. This point, although simple, is subtle. Everyone would agree that patriotism is no excuse for outright fabrication, and that prejudice should never induce a historian to deliberately lie or deceive. Ignatieff's concern, however, was not so much with deliberate falsification as it was with the way prejudice and patriotism can lead to selective perception, which can skew the judgment of even those who are sincere in their efforts to understand the past. The truth, especially about the how and why of historical events, is seldom simple, and those who wish to genuinely understand the past must be sensitive to its complexities.

Each of the anthologies in the Greenhaven Press Interpreting Primary Documents series strives to portray the events and attitudes of the past in all their complexity. Rather than providing a simple narrative of the events, each volume presents a variety of views on the issues and events under discussion and encourages the student to confront and examine the complexity that attends the genuine study of history.

Furthermore, instead of aiming simply to transmit information from historian to student, the series is designed to develop and train students to become historians themselves, by focusing on the interpretation of primary documents. Such documents, including newspaper articles, speeches, personal reflections, letters, diaries, memoranda, and official reports, are the raw material from which the historian refines an authentic understanding of the past. The anthology examining desegregation, for instance, includes the voices of presidents, state governors, and ordinary citizens, and draws from the *Congressional Record*, newspapers and magazines, letters, and books published at the time. The selections differ in scope and opinion as well, allowing the student to examine the issue of desegregation from a variety of perspectives. By looking frankly at the arguments offered by those in favor of racial segregation and by those opposed, for example, students can better understand those arguments, the people who advanced them, and the time in which they lived.

The structure of each book in the Interpreting Primary Documents series helps readers sharpen the critical faculties the serious study of history requires. A concise introduction outlines the era or event at hand and provides the necessary historical background. The chapters themselves begin with a preface containing a straightforward account of the events discussed and an overview of how these events can be interpreted in different ways by examining the different documents in the chapter. The selections, in turn, are chosen for their accessibility and relevance, and each is preceded by a short introduction offering historical context and a summary of the author's point of view. A set of questions to guide interpretation accompanies each article and encourages readers to examine the authors' prejudices, probe their assumptions, and compare and contrast the various perspectives offered in the chapter. Finally, a detailed timeline traces the development of key events, a comprehensive bibliography of selected secondary material guides further research, and a thorough index lets the reader quickly access relevant information.

As Ignatieff remarked, in the same debate in which he urged the historian to favor truth over blind patriotism, "History for me is the study of arguments." The Interpreting Primary Documents series is for readers eager to understand the arguments, and attitudes, that animated historical change.

INTRODUCTION

Racial Segregation in the United States

In the United States, desegregation is intimately connected to the civil rights movement, which shook the country from the mid-1950s to the mid-1970s. Although civil rights activists targeted various forms of racial injustice, one of the most insidious was segregation, the practice of racial separation. The problem was not merely that white and black Americans were kept apart; it was that the public facilities afforded to blacks were almost always inferior. Consequently, segregation perpetuated poverty among black citizens and worked to keep the black population, as a whole, as an underclass, bereft of the rights and opportunities most whites enjoyed. Furthermore, one of the chief purposes of segregation was to enforce an ideology of white supremacy, and in doing so it worked to crush black self-esteem and to foster brutality against black citizens, particularly in the form of lynchings.

Civil rights activists targeted both de jure, or legally enforced, segregation and de facto segregation, which had more to do with custom than with law. The former was prevalent in the southern states, whereas the latter prevailed in the North. In both places, however, in the eyes of those who pushed for an end to segregation and other forms of racial discrimination, Thomas Jefferson's bold declaration, two centuries earlier, that all people have an inalienable right to "life, liberty and the pursuit of happiness," had proven little more than a hollow promise.

At the time Jefferson penned the Declaration of Independence, of course, most blacks in the United States were enslaved. Indeed, segregation was part of the deep legacy of slavery, and in the form attacked by civil rights activists, it for the most part developed only after slavery was abolished at the end of the Civil War. Prior to that, blacks in the South lived overwhelmingly as slaves, subject to the rule of slave owners, so there was little reason for specific laws mandating precisely what blacks could and could not do. Indeed, most of the laws that were the focus of civil rights groups were passed in the last decades of the 1800s, as whites in the South tried to cling to the way of life the Emancipation Proclamation had brought to a close. Similarly, the racial segregation civil rights groups targeted in the North was largely a product of the twentieth century, when hundreds of thousands, if not millions, of emancipated blacks fled the hostile South to seek a better life. Furthermore, the large scale segregation of neighborhoods that marred northern cities only became possible with the advent of automobiles and public transportation systems, which let people live at a distance from their workplace.

A New Kind of Slavery

When the Civil War ended, black men, women, and children in the South, who had done most of the manual work, especially in agriculture, found themselves liberated from two centuries of bondage. White Southerners, however, who controlled all of the capital and resources in the South as well as the state legislatures, quickly reacted to prevent blacks from gaining political or economic ground. Soon, most southern states passed a series of laws known as the black codes, which severely restricted the rights of blacks. In all states, blacks were guaranteed some rights, such as the rights to marry, enter into contracts, own property, and testify against other blacks. Usually, however, black codes set limits on black property ownership and specified that blacks could work only in certain occupations. For instance, in Mississippi blacks could not buy or sell farmland, and in South Carolina blacks needed a license for any work other than agricultural. Furthermore, in most areas interracial marriage, black jury service, and court testimony by blacks against whites was prohibited by law.

Even more odious, perhaps, were laws that promoted an insidious relationship between white law enforcement and white plantation owners. Although blacks were officially free to sign labor contracts with employers, those who did not sign were often fined for vagrancy and "sold" to a plantation owner willing to pay the fine. For instance, the South Carolina Black Code of December 21, 1865, contains the following provisions:

All persons who have not some fixed and known place of abode, and some lawful and reputable employment; those who have not some visible and known means of fair, honest and reputable livelihood; all common prostitutes; those who are found wandering from place to place, vending, bartering, or peddling any articles or commodities, without a license from the District Judge, or other proper authorities; those who, (whether or not they own lands, or are lessees or mechanics), do not provide a reasonable and proper maintenance for themselves and families; those who are engaged in representing publicly or privately, for a fee or reward without license, any tragedy, interlude, comedy, farce, play, or other similar entertainment, exhibition of the circus, sleight of hand, wax work or the like; those who for private gain, without license, give any concert or musical entertainment of any description; fortune tellers; sturdy beggars; common drunkards; those who hunt game of any description, or fish on the land of others, or frequent the premises, contrary to the will of the occupants, shall be deemed vagrants, and be liable to the punishments hereinafter provided. . . . On conviction, the defendant shall be liable to imprisonment, and to hard labor, one or both, as shall be fixed by the verdict, not exceeding twelve months . . . [and may] be hired for such wages as can be obtained for his services . . . [and] the person receiving such vagrant shall have all the rights and remedies for enforcing good conduct and diligence at labor that are herein provided in the case of master and servant.[1]

Although this law and others like it were enacted under the guise of combating vagrancy, in effect blacks were forced to work for whites in conditions very near those of slavery. Despite the promise of emancipation, the situation for blacks had improved only marginally.

An Era of Progress

More substantial improvement came during the period of Reconstruction, which began in 1866 under the northern-dominated Republican Party. In that year, Congress passed a civil rights act, overriding the veto of President Andrew Johnson, that made black men citizens with the same civil rights as all citizens. The passage of the Fourteenth Amendment to the Constitution in 1868 declared that all persons (understood at the time to mean men only) born or naturalized within the United States were citizens deserving equal protection of the law. Although this amendment did not guarantee blacks the right to vote, it provided that any state that prevented black men from voting would lose congressional representation. As a result, blacks were able to influence state legislatures, and within two years, most of the laws that constituted the black codes had been repealed.

The Fifteenth Amendment, which made it illegal to deny suffrage to anyone because of race, color, or previous condition of servitude, was ratified in March 1870. Other important pieces of Reconstruction legislation include three enforcement acts. The first protected black voters, the second provided for federal supervision of elections in the South, and the third, known as the Ku Klux Klan Act, targeted the white supremacist organization, which used violence to intimidate blacks and keep them from voting. Finally, in 1875, Congress passed a major civil rights act that barred discrimination in public facilities and accommodations.

The Reconstruction era was a bright period for blacks in America. In addition to progressive laws, there was a flourishing of black institutions, such as Howard, Atlanta, and Fisk Universities. Reconstruction, however, was as brief as it was promising. By 1877, the Democrats regained control of the South and swiftly enacted laws designed to reverse the liberalizing trend of Reconstruction.

Restrictive Laws

In addition to effectively disenfranchising blacks, state legislatures reversed the progress of Reconstruction by enacting an elaborate series of laws designed to keep blacks and whites separate. The laws, which came to be known as Jim Crow, eventually mandated racial segregation in all walks of life. Racial segregation got a major judicial boost in 1896, when the Supreme Court ruled in *Plessy v. Ferguson* that segregation did not violate the Fourteenth Amendment (which guarantees citizens equal protection of the law) as long as the facilities afforded to blacks and whites were of similar quality. Homer Plessy, a black shoemaker in Louisiana, tested the constitutional basis of the Jim Crow laws. In 1892, he boarded a train and sat in the whites-only section, where he was promptly arrested. The local judge in the case, John Ferguson, rejected Plessy's argument that the Separate Car Act violated the Fourteenth Amendment and held that Louisiana had the right to prevent racial mixing within its borders. In Ferguson's opinion, the Fourteenth Amendment guaranteed only legal equality, not social equality. Upon appeal, the Louisiana Supreme Court agreed, as did the U.S. Supreme Court in its 1896 ruling. The lone dissenting voice was that of Supreme Court Justice John Marshall Harlan, who insisted that the Constitution was color-blind and predicted that the judgment would provoke racial hatred:

The present decision, it may well be apprehended, will not only stimulate aggressions, more or less brutal and irritating, upon the admitted rights of colored citizens, but will encourage the belief that it is possible, by means of state enactments, to defeat the beneficent purposes which the people of the United States had in view when they adopted the recent amendments of the Constitution, by one of which the blacks of this country were made citizens of the United States and of the States in which they respectively reside, and whose privileges and immunities, as citizens, the States are forbidden to abridge. . . . The destinies of the two races in this country are indissolubly linked together, and the interests of both require that the common government of all shall not permit the seeds of race hate to be planted under the sanction of law. What can more certainly arouse race hate, what more certainly create and perpetuate a feeling of distrust between these races, than state enactments, which, in fact, proceed on the ground that colored citizens are so inferior and degraded that they cannot be allowed to sit in public coaches occupied by white citizens?[2]

However prescient Harlan's opinion may have been, it was his alone. The "separate but equal" doctrine established by the majority of the Court effectively gave state legislatures in the South carte blanche to segregate, and sanctioned racially discriminatory laws for the next sixty years.

The Growth of Segregation
The move toward full segregation was not immediate, but it was inexorable. As early as 1881, Tennessee had segregated railroad cars, and by 1907 there were similar laws in Florida, Mississippi, Texas, Louisiana, Alabama, Kentucky, Arkansas, Georgia, South Carolina, North Carolina, Virginia, Maryland, and Oklahoma. In 1910, the city council in Baltimore, Maryland, officially set out the boundaries of black and white neighborhoods, and similar ordinances followed in other southern cities. In 1913, the federal government began to segregate many of its own workplaces, rest

rooms, and lunchrooms. In 1914, a Louisiana law required separate entrances at circuses. The following year, Oklahoma segregated telephone booths. In 1920, Mississippi made it illegal to advocate social equality for blacks or racial intermarriage. By the Second World War, every school, university, hotel, train, waiting room, public washroom, restaurant, elevator, drinking fountain, swimming pool, prison, church, and cemetery in the South was segregated.

Although such de jure segregation took place in the South, it had a huge effect on the North, and helped produce de facto segregation there. In the early part of the twentieth century, especially after the First World War, blacks migrated in huge numbers from the rural South into the great cities of the North. Many moved to escape the discrimination of Jim Crow and the violence and intimidation perpetrated by such groups as the Ku Klux Klan. (Between 1884 and 1920, for instance, more than three thousand black men were lynched in the South.) The economic opportunities offered by the urban, industrialized centers of the North were also a strong draw, as was the relatively open and exciting culture of cities such as New York and Chicago. Such migration swelled the ranks of the black population in the North, and led to the development of distinctively black neighborhoods in northern cities. Furthermore, the advent of bus, streetcar, and subway transportation made it easier for residential segregation to develop.

A Racially Divided North
Soon, although no signs or laws designated certain places "whites only" or "colored," segregation was a fact of life in the North. The core was residential segregation, which was helped along by real estate agents, banks, and urban planners. Black homeowners would typically be shown only homes in all-black neighborhoods, and banks were often reluctant to finance mortgages for blacks considering a home in a white part of town. Urban planners contributed to residential segregation because they decided where to put streets, highways, and access ramps, and thus con-

trolled the flow of traffic within a city. It soon became easy for whites, zipping along a highway, to bypass black areas of town, and blacks often had limited access to white neighborhoods. Urban planners also decided on the development, location, and extent of new residential, commercial, and industrial areas. Furthermore, because of a considerable income gap between whites and blacks, class segregation tended to manifest as racial segregation. Sometimes insidiously, sometimes unwittingly, black and white neighborhoods in the North were gradually cut off from each other as cities expanded.

This de facto residential segregation led to school segregation. Children attended neighborhood schools, which meant that if they lived in all-black neighborhoods, they attended all-black schools. Furthermore, despite the progressive image the North projected, school districts were sometimes drawn up in a way that was designed to keep whites and blacks apart. The segregation intensified after the Second World War, when more and more whites left the cities for the rapidly developing suburbs, where new single-family homes were abundant. For the predominately white middle class capable of affording such a home, life in the expansive suburbs had much to offer over city life. This was especially so for whites who were uneasy about the growing black population in northern cities. This white migration to the suburbs is often called the "white flight."

The differences between segregation in the southern states and in the northern states were well captured by the U.S. Commission on Civil Rights, which issued a report titled *Freedom to the Free* in 1963. It described those differences as follows:

In the South, the problem may be characterized generally as resistance to the established law of the land and to social change. The irresistible force is moving the object which was thought to be immovable; progress is slow and often painful, but it is steady and it appears to be inevitable. In the North, the issue is not one of resistance to law. It is here that segregation and discrimination are usually *de facto* rather than *de jure*, and it is here that the last battle for equal rights may be fought in America. The "gentlemen's agreement" that bars the minority citizen from housing outside the ghetto; the employment practices that often hold him in a menial status, regardless of his capabilities; and the overburdened neighborhood schools, which deprive him of an adequate education, despite his ambitions—these are the subtler forms of denial and the more difficult to eliminate.[3]

Segregation was much less obvious in the North, and the more extreme displays of racism common below the Mason-Dixon Line were largely absent. Nonetheless, even though whites in the North were generally opposed to the legal segregation mandated in the South, they were much less eager to embrace integration in their communities and schools.

Voices for Change

Although blacks faced many new challenges in the decades following the end of Reconstruction, those decades also saw the rise of a new racial consciousness among blacks, which was to later culminate in the modern civil rights movement. There had long been black activists, but they gained a new prominence after emancipation. Some, such as Booker T. Washington, were popular among whites because they pushed a moderate platform that emphasized patience in the face of discrimination. Others, such as W.E.B. Du Bois, rejected this policy of gradualism and demanded full civil rights and social equality for blacks. One of the most important organizations was the National Association for the Advancement of Colored People (NAACP), which was founded in 1909. Bringing together a group of black activists organized by Du Bois and progressive whites headed by the grandson of abolitionist William Lloyd Garrison, the association focused on providing legal assistance to blacks in southern states and challenging discriminatory laws on constitutional grounds. Other important organizations were the Brotherhood of Sleeping Car Porters, a black labor union, and the Universal Negro Improvement Organization, a popular black nationalist group founded by Marcus Garvey with headquarters in New York City.

Until the Second World War, progress on desegregation and other civil rights issues came slowly. In 1917, the Supreme Court found in *Buchanan v. Warley* that a Louisville, Kentucky, ordinance mandating segregated neighborhoods was unconstitutional. In the early 1930s, a group of black lawyers led by Charles Houston, vice dean of law at Howard University, and Thurgood Marshall, one of his students who would later become the first black justice on the Supreme Court, began targeting segregation laws with earnest. In 1935, in *Hollins v. Oklahoma*, the Supreme Court ruled that blacks could not be excluded from jury duty. In 1938, the Court ruled in *Gaines v. Canada* that Missouri had to either integrate state law schools or build a law school for blacks. And the following year, First Lady Eleanor Roosevelt took a stand against segregation by publicly resigning from the Daughters of the American Revolution, a group that had blocked the black singer Marian Anderson from giving a concert at Constitution Hall. At the invitation of Secretary of the Interior Harold L. Ickes, Anderson later gave a concert on the steps of the Lincoln Memorial, the symbolism of which was apparent to most observers.

During and after the Second World War, which pitted the United States and its allies against the racist Nazis, progress on civil rights increased. Membership in the NAACP swelled tenfold, and by the end of the war stood at nearly 500,000. Asa Philip Randolph, the leader of the Brotherhood of Sleeping Car Porters, convinced the federal government during the war to end discrimination in government departments and in army, navy, air corps, and defense jobs by threatening a massive march in Washington. And the Congress on Racial Equality, inspired by the Indian spiritual leader Mohandas Gandhi, who successfully confronted British imperialism with the method of nonviolent resistance, began using the technique to desegregate public facilities in Detroit, Denver, and Chicago. In addition, during the war, nearly 1 million black men and women served in the armed forces, and although almost all units were segregated, and racial violence was not uncommon, combat needs slowly extended the range of military opportunities open to blacks.

The Pace of Desegregation Quickens

In 1947, integration reached the masses when Jackie Robinson became the first black player in Major League Baseball. That same year, the President's Committee on Civil Rights, which had been commissioned by President Harry S. Truman, released a report cataloging and criticizing pervasive discrimination in the United States. In response, Truman issued an executive order desegregating the armed forces and formed the Fair Employment Practices Commission, which worked to ensure that blacks had an equal chance at securing federal jobs. The trend toward desegregation continued in 1950 when the Supreme Court issued two important rulings on segregation in state-supported law and doctoral programs. In *Sweatt v. Painter,* the court mandated that the University of Texas Law School admit black students, holding that Herman Sweatt was denied an equal educational opportunity in the law school for blacks. In *McLaurin v. Oklahoma State Regents,* the Court similarly ruled that John McLaurin, a black doctoral student, was being denied an equal education because he was forced to sit in a special "colored" section of classrooms and at a special table in the library and cafeteria. Both rulings relied on the 1896 *Plessy v. Ferguson* judgment, which had held that segregation was constitutional as long as equality was preserved. That historic precedent, which had given legal sanction to nearly sixty years of segregation, would itself fall four years later in the landmark case *Brown v. Board of Education of Topeka, Kansas.*

The *Brown* case concerned Linda Brown, a black student who was bused across town to a black school even though she lived near a white school. The Supreme Court ruled, unanimously, that school segregation violated the Fourteenth Amendment's guarantee of equal protection of the law. Separating black schoolchildren from their white peers, the Court found, inculcates in them feelings of inferiority and thus harms their educational opportunities. "In the field of public education, the doctrine of 'separate but equal' has no place," the Court concluded. "Separate education facilities are inherently unequal."[4] The following year, the Court issued its compliance ruling, ordering southern states to integrate "with all deliberate speed."[5]

A Refusal to Comply

The *Brown* ruling went far beyond earlier judgments in education cases by outlawing all segregation in the public school system. The most northern of the southern states soon complied with the Court's ruling by quietly integrating, and Washington, D.C., integrated under order of President Dwight D. Eisenhower. In the Deep South, however, state and local officials made no move to integrate, and soon made it clear that they had no intention of doing so. Instead, they adopted policies of massive resistance and interposition, according to which they used various means, legal and illegal, to resist implementing the federal ruling. In 1956, one hundred members of Congress signed a declaration calling the Supreme Court ruling an "unwarranted exercise of power by the Court, contrary to the Constitution,"[6] and when the year closed, not a single school in the Deep South was integrated.

Southern resistance to school integration continued for several years, and on numerous occasions involved the use of state force. In 1957, for instance, Arkansas governor Orval Faubus ordered the Arkansas National Guard to surround Little Rock Central High School, which was to be integrated by nine black students, ostensibly to keep the peace. It soon became clear, however, that his real purpose was to defy federal desegregation orders. The tense situation continued until an angry crowd of whites, numbering nearly one thousand, replaced the National Guard, which had been withdrawn under court order. President Eisenhower took the Guard under his command and ordered it to protect the students. Even this, however, was not enough to ensure integration. Governor Faubus closed down the high schools of Little Rock in 1958 and 1959, and when the decade closed, less than 1 percent of black students in the South attended integrated schools.

National Guardsmen were again deployed under federal command in an effort to ensure desegregation five years after the Little Rock incident. In September 1962, riots broke out at the University of Mississippi when James Meredith arrived on campus with a Supreme Court order guaranteeing him admission. President John F. Kennedy ordered the Mississippi National Guard to keep the peace. In June of the following year, Kennedy ordered the Alabama National Guard to assist in the integration of the University of Alabama after the state governor, George C. Wallace, positioned himself in the door of the registration office with a pledge to personally block the entry of two black students. That evening, Kennedy spoke to the nation on radio and television, calling racism and segregation clear moral wrongs and urging Congress to pass substantial civil rights laws.

The Montgomery Bus Boycott

Although the desegregation of schools was a priority for civil rights activists, equally urgent were the calls for an end to segregation in other public facilities. In December 1955, the same year that the Supreme Court ruled that school desegregation was to proceed "with all deliberate speed," the arrest of Rosa Parks set off a major bus boycott in Montgomery, Alabama. Parks had refused to vacate her bus seat for a white passenger, and after her arrest, black community leaders hastily organized the Montgomery Improvement Association, with Martin Luther King Jr. as its president, to manage a boycott. The boycott lasted over a year, until the Supreme Court ordered the bus system to integrate.

Segregated transportation was again the focus of a

Supreme Court ruling in 1960, when the nation's highest court held in *Boynton v. Virginia* that segregation in interstate bus and railroad facilities was illegal. The following year, the Congress of Racial Equality launched the Freedom Rides, in which integrated buses were to travel from Washington, D.C., to New Orleans to test compliance with the ruling. One bus was attacked and burned by angry whites in Montgomery, Alabama, and in Birmingham, Alabama, riders were severely beaten by a white mob while police stood by and watched.

Segregated businesses were another important target of civil rights activists. Beginning in Greensboro, North Carolina, a wave of sit-in protests led by students and other young people captured national media attention and led to the integration of restaurants, hotels, department stores, and other places of business. In such protests, black students, having been trained to remain calm and poised despite great provocation, would peacefully and patiently await service at white-only businesses, despite fierce taunting by angry white onlookers. Such protests often ended with the arrests of those participating, and thousands of blacks and their white allies served time in jail for their part in the protests.

One particularly marked example of zealous policing occurred in Birmingham, Alabama, in the spring of 1963, when hundreds of demonstrators gathered to march on city hall, picket stores, and stage sit-in protests. Local police used dogs and fire hoses to disperse the demonstrators and made mass arrests, filling local jails with marchers, many of whom were children. State troopers also attacked civil rights demonstrators outside Selma, Alabama, in 1965 at the start of a march demanding voting rights; the Ku Klux Klan murdered several of the marchers.

The Rejection of Violence

The motivating principle behind much of the protest in the South was the philosophy of nonviolent resistance, which was adopted from Gandhi and championed most prominently in the United States by Martin Luther King Jr. The idea was that by breaking unjust laws and allowing oneself to be arrested or brutalized by police or onlookers, one could highlight the prevailing injustice of racism. Furthermore, by remaining nonviolent, even when met with violence, protesters drew the sympathy and support of countless white Americans, especially in the North, who watched the events on their television screens. As Martin Luther King Jr. put it,

> The method of non-violent resistance is effective in that it has a way of disarming opponents. It exposes their moral defenses, weakens their morale and at the same time works on their conscience. It makes it possible for the individual to struggle for moral ends through moral means. . . . It is the method which seeks to implement just law by appealing to the conscience of the great decent majority who through blindness, fear, pride or irrationality have allowed their consciences to sleep.[7]

Although not everyone involved in the nonviolence movement was Christian, many were, so there tended to be a heavy emphasis on Christian ideals of pacifism and brotherly love.

In 1964, Congress passed the most important piece of civil rights legislation since Reconstruction, and the most sweeping and powerful legislative protection of civil rights ever proposed. At the time, the Fourteenth Amendment, which guarantees citizens equal protection of the law, was interpreted to block only discrimination by the government. In order to reach private discrimination by individuals, Congress used its power to regulate interstate commerce and enacted the Civil Rights Act of 1964. As the Senate Minority Leader Everett Dirksen of Illinois said at the time, "This is an idea whose time has come. It will not be stayed. It will not be denied."[8] The Civil Rights Act of 1964 bars discrimination based on "race, color, religion, or national origin" in public establishments connected to interstate commerce or supported by the state. Consequently, segregation in hotels, restaurants, bars, gas stations, and most places of entertainment became illegal. Title VII of the act also barred discrimination in companies engaged in interstate commerce with more than fifteen employees. By 1968, new statute law, in concert with judicial rulings, had ended all de jure segregation, and considerable progress had been made in integrating schools in southern states, which had abandoned the early policy of massive resistance.

Desegregating the North

Many white citizens in the North had watched the desegregation movement in the South with a mix of smugness and horror. Northern states had long been free of the overt racism and de jure segregation that plagued the South, and most whites were sympathetic to the black cause. Soon, however, the focus of civil rights activists shifted to the northern states, where de facto segregation and poverty reigned in black communities. Here, the problems seemed deeper, and more subtle. In a commencement address at Howard University in 1965, President Lyndon B. Johnson remarked on these lingering problems:

> Of course Negro Americans as well as white Americans have shared in our rising national abundance. But the harsh fact of the matter is that in the battle for true equality too many are losing ground. We are not completely sure why this is. The causes are complex and subtle. But we do know the two broad basic reasons. And we know we have to act.
>
> First, Negroes are trapped—as many whites are trapped—in inherited, gateless poverty. They lack training and skills. They are shut in slums, without decent medical care. Private and public poverty combine to cripple their capacities. . . . But there is a second cause— more difficult to explain, more deeply grounded, more desperate in its force. It is the devastating heritage of

long years of slavery; and a century of oppression, hatred and injustice.

For Negro poverty is not white poverty. Many of its causes and many of its cures are the same. But there are differences—deep, corrosive, obstinate differences—radiating painful roots into the community, the family, and the nature of the individual. These differences are not racial differences. They are solely and simply the consequence of ancient brutality, past injustice, and present prejudice. . . . Nor can these differences be understood as isolated infirmities. They are a seamless web. They cause each other. They result from each other. Much of the Negro community is buried under a blanket of history and circumstance. It is not a lasting solution to lift just one corner.[9]

Although Johnson called for renewing vigor on the issue of combating racial discrimination and inequality, progress came slowly, especially after the enormous expense of the Vietnam War diverted funds from domestic projects. In addition to affirmative action, which sought to desegregate universities and workplaces by encouraging the hiring of blacks, courts ordered busing of schoolchildren in an effort to overcome residential segregation. The idea of busing children to school in a way that was designed to ensure adequate racial mixing originated in the South, where it was done to overcome decades of de jure segregation. In 1971, the Supreme Court ruled in *Swann v. Charlotte-Mecklenburg* that schools where such segregation had existed were to use any means necessary, including busing, to integrate. Two years later, in *Keyes v. Denver,* the Supreme Court mandated similar steps in the North if school segregation could be attributed to public policy. Soon, busing was common around the country, much to the consternation of most whites. In fact, Boston became known as "the Little Rock of the North" after violent protests, which were seen to echo the 1957 protests in Little Rock, Arkansas, broke out over busing in 1974. Eventually, however, busing was accepted in most cities, and it continued for the most part well into the 1990s.

The Movement Slows

Most historians believe that the mid-1960s were the highwater mark for the civil rights movement and that throughout the 1970s the movement lost momentum. The reasons for this are complex. They have to do with the assassinations of Martin Luther King Jr., Malcolm X, and Robert Kennedy, each of whom was a key figure in the civil rights movement; a shift of national attention toward the Vietnam War; and the more intractable nature of the problems revealed when the movement shifted to the North. The election of Richard Nixon, who opposed busing and was attacked by the U.S. Civil Rights Commission for weak enforcement of civil rights legislation, also marked a turning point in federal support for desegregation initiatives. Nixon appointed four justices to the U.S. Supreme Court, leading to key 5–4 decisions against desegregation across city-suburban lines (*Milliken v. Bradley*, 1974) and against equalizing finances among school districts (*San Antonio Independent School District v. Rodriguez*, 1973).

It is not easy to assess the long-term effect of the civil rights movement and the push to end racial segregation. On one hand, it is clear that the letter of the law permits no racial discrimination and that white racism has steadily declined throughout the United States since the 1950s. It is also clear that students at integrated schools perform better academically and are more likely to go to college. In fact, a recent study showed that almost all of the black and Hispanic students at elite law schools in the United States come from integrated schools. Furthermore, polls show that most people in the country, regardless of race, favor integrated education. Although this suggests that the drive for desegregation was successful, in recent years the Supreme Court, once a strong force for desegregation, has favored a different approach to racial issues. Under Justice William Rehnquist, who as a law clerk at the time of

Brown v. Board of Education urged that the "separate but equal" doctrine be continued, the Court found that there was a serious danger of discrimination against whites if civil rights requirements, particularly in regard to busing, were to continue. Reflecting appointments by Presidents Richard Nixon, Ronald Reagan, and George H.W. Bush, three judgments in the 1990s released school boards from various desegregation obligations. Furthermore, in recent years, social scientists and journalists have documented increasing racial segregation in the nation's neighborhoods and schools, which suggests that the desegregation advances may have been only partial victories.

Notes

1. South Carolina Black Code, December 21, 1865, *Acts of the General Assembly of the State of South Carolina, 1864–1865,* pp. 291–304.

2. *Plessy v. Ferguson,* 163 U.S. 537 (1896). http://laws.findlaw.com.

3. *Freedom to the Free,* report to the president of the U.S. Commission on Civil Rights. Washington, DC: U.S. Government Printing Office, 1963, p. 205.

4. *Brown v. Board of Education,* 347 U.S. 483 (1954). http://supreme.lp.findlaw.com.

5. *Brown v. Board of Education,* 349 U.S. 294 (1955). http://supreme.lp.findlaw.com.

6. *Congressional Record, 84th Congress, Second Session,* vol. 102, part 4, March 12, 1956. Washington, DC: U.S. Government Printing Office, 1956, p. 4,459.

7. Quoted in Anthony Lewis and the *New York Times, Portrait of a Decade: The Second American Revolution.* New York: Random House, 1964, pp. 98–99.

8. Quoted in Albert P. Blaustein and Robert L. Zangrando, eds., *Civil Rights and the American Negro: A Documentary History.* New York: Washington Square Press, 1968, p. 525.

9. Lyndon B. Johnson, "Commencement Address at Howard University, 'To Fulfill These Rights,' June 4, 1965," *Public Papers of the Presidents of the United States: Lyndon B. Johnson, 1965,* vol. 2, entry 301, pp. 635–40.

CHAPTER

1

THE WINDS
OF CHANGE

CHAPTER PREFACE

Although few people today believe that racial segregation is desirable, this was not the case a half-century ago, especially in the southern states, where de jure, or legally enforced, segregation was the norm. That system of racial segregation, known as Jim Crow, developed after slavery was abolished, when whites, deeply resentful of the sudden emancipation of their slaves, enacted a series of laws that were designed to preserve a semblance of antebellum life. In the last decades of the nineteenth century and the first few decades of the twentieth, there existed in the South an elaborate, hierarchical social arrangement in which, by and large, black Americans and white Americans lived in separate social spheres. Both law and custom—and on occasion white violence, particularly lynching—preserved this social arrangement. Although there were certainly poor whites, in general, whites tended to be more affluent and more likely to own property, whereas blacks, again with some exceptions, tended to populate the laboring class, working in menial agricultural, domestic, service, or industrial jobs. Furthermore, the legacy of slavery was strong; education and literacy were much lower among the black population than among the white, which only served to worsen the prejudices and fears of white Southerners. It is against this background that the desegregation struggle, and the larger civil rights movement of which it is a part, took place.

That struggle and movement, which reached its peak in the years between 1954 and 1965, was not a spontaneous event but the culmination of a long natural progression. One important step in that progression was the 1947 publication of *To Secure These Rights* by the President's Committee on Civil Rights. This report, commissioned by President Harry S. Truman, was a sweeping indictment of the status quo in America. It pointed to deep and pervasive discrimination throughout the country, argued that it came at high social and economic cost, and emphasized that it stood in sharp contrast to American ideals preached abroad. These same considerations feature in the arguments of Benjamin E. Mays, who insists, contrary to much of the prevailing sentiment of the day, that segregation is a deep moral wrong. As Mays sees it, segregation is neither natural nor desirable, for it harms black citizens and offends their human dignity. Thus, one way of interpreting the growing call for greater rights for black Americans was as a justified response to a moral outrage; this was the response of Mays and, somewhat more cautiously, of the President's Committee.

A quite different view of desegregation is offered by James Jackson Kilpatrick, a prominent southern newspaper editor at the time. In contrast to Mays and the President's Committee, Kilpatrick thinks that racial segregation is appropriate. He insists—and argues that almost all white Southerners insist—that a basic premise of those in favor of desegregation is false. Whites, as a race, are superior to blacks, as a race, according to Kilpatrick, and, as he sees it, this justifies the need for racial separation. Finally, a third view of the looming change is offered by Lenoir Chambers, another southern newspaper editor. Chambers argues that, however strong the reasons in favor of segregation may be, the winds of change cannot be resisted; he urges white Southerners to accept change and adapt accordingly.

Although these views do not exhaust the possible views one could have on the subject of racial segregation, they touch on the core issues involved. Is segregation morally wrong, and if so, why? What were the economic costs or benefits of segregation, and to whom? Was desegregation in the United States an isolated occurrence, or did it reflect, and perhaps even strengthen, a general international trend toward liberty, equality, and self-determination? What does it mean to speak of inherent racial equality, and does desegregation, or do civil rights, indeed depend on racial equality? And finally, how do citizens adjust and adapt to deep change in their society and in their ways of life?

The Time for Change Is Now

The President's Committee on Civil Rights

The following is excerpted from a 1947 report by the President's Committee on Civil Rights. This influential study documented civil rights abuses in the United States, including segregation, and argued that there were moral, economic, and international reasons for change. In terms of moral reasons, the report found that the American values of liberty and equality were better preached than practiced. In terms of economic reasons, the report found that pervasive discrimination worked to keep blacks poor, and thus harmed the economy. The authors of the report also express their view that economic hardship and general ill-treatment by whites fosters aggression in blacks and leads to social withdrawal, which damages the "human wealth" in the United States. Finally, by way of international reasons, the report notes that accusations of hypocrisy and negative reactions to American prejudice impede the achievement of American foreign policy goals. The report, which was commissioned under President Harry S. Truman, gave a significant boost to civil rights and desegregation efforts, which were pursued with renewed earnest in the years immediately following the report's publication.

As you read, consider the following questions:
1. Why do the authors include, in addition to moral reasons, economic and international reasons?
2. The authors of the report consistently point to the harm segregation does to the country as a whole, rather than to merely the harm done to individual citizens. What reasons could they have for doing this?

Excerpted from "To Secure These Rights," by the President's Committee on Civil Rights, *Debating the Civil Rights Movement 1945–1968*, edited by Steven F. Lawson and Charles Payne (New York: Rowman and Littlefield, 1998).

3. Are the arguments the report offers compelling? Why or why not?

Twice before in American history the nation has found it necessary to review the state of its civil rights. The first time was during the 15 years between 1776 and 1791, from the drafting of the Declaration of Independence through the Articles of Confederation experiment to the writing of the Constitution and the Bill of Rights. It was then that the distinctively American heritage was finally distilled from earlier views of liberty. The second time was when the Union was temporarily sundered over the question of whether it could exist "half-slave" and "half-free."

It is our profound conviction that we have come to a time for a third re-examination of the situation, and a sustained drive ahead. Our reasons for believing this are those of conscience, of self-interest, and of survival in a threatening world. Or to put it another way, we have a moral reason, an economic reason, and an international reason for believing that the time for action is now.

The Moral Reason

We have considered the American heritage of freedom at some length. We need no further justification for a broad and immediate program than the need to reaffirm our faith in the traditional American morality. The pervasive gap between our aims and what we actually do is creating a kind of moral dry rot which eats away at the emotional and rational basis of democratic beliefs. There are times when the difference between what we preach about civil rights and what we practice is shockingly illustrated by individual outrages. There are times when the whole structure of our ideology is made ridiculous by individual instances. And there are certain continuing, quiet, omnipresent practices which do irreparable damage to our beliefs.

As examples of "moral erosion" there are the consequences of suffrage limitations in the South. The fact that

Negroes and many whites have not been allowed to vote in some states has actually sapped the morality underlying universal suffrage. Many men in public and private life do not believe that those who have been kept from voting are capable of self rule. They finally convince themselves that disfranchised people do not really have the right to vote.

Wartime segregation in the armed forces is another instance of how a social pattern may wreak moral havoc. Practically all white officers and enlisted men in all branches of service saw Negro military personnel performing only the most menial functions. They saw Negroes recruited for the common defense treated as men apart and distinct from themselves. As a result, men who might otherwise have maintained the equalitarian morality of their forebears were given reason to look down on their fellow citizens. This has been sharply illustrated by the Army study discussed previously, in which white servicemen expressed great surprise at the excellent performance of Negroes who joined them in the firing line. Even now, very few people know of the successful experiment with integrated combat units. Yet it is important in explaining why some Negro troops did not do well; it is proof that equal treatment can produce equal performance.

Unfair Play

Thousands upon thousands of small, unseen incidents reinforce the impact of headlined violations like lynchings, and broad social patterns like segregation and inequality of treatment. There is, for example, the matter of "fair play." As part of its training for democratic life, our youth is constantly told to "play fair," to abide by "the rules of the game," and to be "good sports." Yet, how many boys and girls in our country experience such things as Washington's annual marble tournament? Because of the prevailing pattern of segregation, established as a model for youth in the schools and recreation systems, separate tournaments are held for Negro and white boys. Parallel elimination contests are sponsored until only two victors remain. Without a contest between them, the white boy is automatically designated as the local champion and sent to the national tournament, while the Negro lad is relegated to the position of runner-up. What child can achieve any real understanding of fair play, or sportsmanship, of the rules of the game, after he has personally experienced such an example of inequality?

It is impossible to decide who suffers the greatest moral damage from our civil rights transgressions, because all of us are hurt. That is certainly true of those who are victimized. Their belief in the basic truth of the American promise is undermined. But they do have the realization, galling as it sometimes is, of being morally in the right. The damage to those who are responsible for these violations of our moral standards may well be greater. They, too, have been reared to honor the command of "free and equal." And all of us must share in the shame at the growth of hypocrisies like the "automatic" marble champion. All of us must endure the cynicism about democratic values which our failures breed.

The United States can no longer countenance these burdens on its common conscience, these inroads on its moral fiber.

The Economic Reason

One of the principal economic problems facing us and the rest of the world is achieving maximum production and continued prosperity. The loss of a huge, potential market for goods is a direct result of the economic discrimination which is practiced against many of our minority groups. A sort of vicious circle is produced. Discrimination depresses the wages and income of minority groups. As a result, their purchasing power is curtailed and markets are reduced. Reduced markets result in reduced production. This cuts down employment, which of course means lower wages and still fewer job opportunities. Rising fear, prejudice, and insecurity aggravate the very discrimination in employment which sets the vicious circle in motion.

Minority groups are not the sole victims of this economic waste; its impact is inevitably felt by the entire population. Eric Johnston, when President of the United States Chamber of Commerce, made this point with vividness and clarity:

> The withholding of jobs and business opportunities from some people does not make more jobs and business opportunities for others. Such a policy merely tends to drag down the whole economic level. You can't sell an electric refrigerator to a family that can't afford electricity. Perpetuating poverty for some merely guarantees stagnation for all. True economic progress demands that the whole nation move forward at the same time. It demands that all artificial barriers erected by ignorance and intolerance be removed. To put it in the simplest terms, we are all in business together. Intolerance is a species of boycott and any business or job boycott is a cancer in the economic body of the nation. I repeat, intolerance is destructive; prejudice produces no wealth; discrimination is a fool's economy.

Economic discrimination prevents full use of all our resources. During the war, when we were called upon to make an all-out productive effort, we found that we lacked skilled laborers. This shortage might not have been so serious if minorities had not frequently been denied opportunities for training and experience. In the end, it cost large amounts of money and precious time to provide ourselves with trained persons.

Discrimination imposes a direct cost upon our economy through the wasteful duplication of many facilities and services required by the "separate but equal" policy. That the resources of the South are sorely strained by the burden of a double system of schools and other public services has already been indicated. Segregation is also economically wasteful for private business. Public transportation companies must often provide duplicate facilities to serve majority and minority groups separately. Places of public accommodation and recreation reject business when it comes in the form of unwanted persons. Stores reduce their sales by turning away minority customers. Factories must provide separate locker rooms, pay windows, drinking fountains, and washrooms for the different groups.

Discrimination in wage scales and hiring policies forces a higher proportion of some minority groups onto relief rolls than corresponding segments of the majority. . . .

The Social Costs

Similarly, the rates of disease, crime, and fires are disproportionately great in areas which are economically depressed as compared with wealthier areas. Many of the prominent American minorities are confined—by economic discrimination, by law, by restrictive covenants, and by social pressure—to the most dilapidated, undesirable locations. Property in these locations yields a smaller return in taxes, which is seldom sufficient to meet the inordinately high cost of public services in depressed areas. The majority pays a high price in taxes for the low status of minorities.

To the costs of discrimination must be added the expensive investigations, trials, and property losses which result from civil rights violations. In the aggregate, these attain huge proportions. The 1943 Detroit riot alone resulted in the destruction of two million dollars in property.

Finally, the cost of prejudice cannot be computed in terms of markets, production, and expenditures. Perhaps the most expensive results are the least tangible ones. No nation can afford to have its component groups hostile toward one another without feeling the stress. People who live in a state of tension and suspicion cannot use their energy constructively. The frustrations of their restricted existence are translated into aggression against the dominant group. [Gunnar] Myrdal says:

> Not only occasional acts of violence, but most laziness, carelessness, unreliability, petty stealing and ly-

ing are undoubtedly to be explained as concealed aggression. . . . The truth is that *Negroes generally do not feel they have unqualified moral obligations to white people.* . . . The voluntary withdrawal which has intensified the isolation between the two castes is also an expression of Negro protest under cover.

It is not at all surprising that a people relegated to second-class citizenship should behave as second-class citizens. This is true, in varying degrees, of all of our minorities. What we have lost in money, production, invention, citizenship, and leadership as the price for damaged, thwarted personalities—these are beyond estimate.

The United States can no longer afford this heavy drain upon its human wealth, its national competence.

The International Reason

Our position in the postwar world is so vital to the future that our smallest actions have far-reaching effects. We have come to know that our own security in a highly interdependent world is inextricably tied to the security and well-being of all people and all countries. Our foreign policy is designed to make the United States an enormous, positive influence for peace and progress throughout the world. We have tried to let nothing, not even extreme political differences between ourselves and foreign nations, stand in the way of this goal. But our domestic civil rights shortcomings are a serious obstacle.

In a letter to the Fair Employment Practice Committee on May 8, 1946, the Honorable Dean Acheson, then Acting Secretary of State, stated that:

. . . the existence of discrimination against minority groups in this country has an adverse effect upon our relations with other countries. We are reminded over and over by some foreign newspapers and spokesmen, that our treatment of various minorities leaves much to be desired. While sometimes these pronouncements are exaggerated and unjustified, they all too frequently point with accuracy to some form of discrimination because of race, creed, color, or national origin. Frequently we find it next to impossible to formulate a satisfactory answer to our critics in other countries; the gap between the things we stand for in principle and the facts of a particular situation may be too wide to be bridged. An atmosphere of suspicion and resentment in a country over the way a minority is being treated in the United States is a formidable obstacle to the development of mutual understanding and trust between the two countries. We will have better international relations when these reasons for suspicion and resentment have been removed.

I think it is quite obvious . . . that the existence of discriminations against minority groups in the United States is a handicap in our relations with other countries. The Department of State, therefore, has good reason to hope for the continued and increased effectiveness of public and private efforts to do away with these discriminations.

The people of the United States stem from many lands. Other nations and their citizens are naturally intrigued by what has happened to their American "relatives." Discrimination against, or mistreatment of, any racial, religious or national group in the United States is not only seen as our internal problem. The dignity of a country, a continent, or even a major portion of the world's population, may be outraged by it. A relatively few individuals here may be identified with millions of people elsewhere, and the way in which they are treated may have world-wide repercussions. We have fewer than half a million American Indians; there are 30 million more in the Western Hemisphere. Our Mexican American and Hispano groups are not large; millions in Central and South America consider them kin. We number our citizens of Oriental descent in the hundreds of thousands; their counterparts overseas are numbered in hundreds of millions. Throughout the Pacific, Latin America, Africa, the Near, Middle, and Far East, the treatment which our Negroes receive is taken as a reflection of our attitudes toward all dark-skinned peoples.

Confronting Prejudice

In the recent war, citizens of a dozen European nations were happy to meet Smiths, Cartiers, O'Haras, Schultzes, di Salvos, Cohens, and Sklodowskas and all the others in our armies. Each nation could share in our victories because its "sons" had helped win them. How much of this good feeling was dissipated when they found virulent prejudice among some of our troops is impossible to say.

We cannot escape the fact that our civil rights record has been an issue in world politics. The world's press and radio are full of it. This Committee has seen a multitude of samples. We and our friends have been, and are, stressing our achievements. Those with competing philosophies have stressed—and are shamelessly distorting—our shortcomings. They have not only tried to create hostility toward us among specific nations, races, and religious groups. They have tried to prove our democracy an empty fraud, and our nation a consistent oppressor of underprivileged people. This may seem ludicrous to Americans, but it is sufficiently important to worry our friends. The following United Press dispatch from London proves that (*Washington Post*, May 25, 1947):

> Although the Foreign Office reserved comment on recent lynch activities in the Carolinas, British diplomatic circles said privately today that they have played into the hands of Communist propagandists in Europe. . . .

> Diplomatic circles said the two incidents of mob violence would provide excellent propaganda ammunition for Communist agents who have been decrying America's brand of "freedom" and "democracy."

News of the North Carolina kidnapping was prominently displayed by London papers. . . .

The international reason for acting to secure our civil rights now is not to win the approval of our totalitarian critics. We would not expect it if our record were spotless; to them our civil rights record is only a convenient weapon with which to attack us. Certainly we would like to deprive them of that weapon. But we are more concerned with the good opinion of the peoples of the world. Our achievements in building and maintaining a state dedicated to the fundamentals of freedom have already served as a guide for those seeking the best road from chaos to liberty and prosperity. But it is not indelibly written that democracy will encompass the world. We are convinced that our way of life—the free way of life—holds a promise of hope for all people. We have what is perhaps the greatest responsibility ever placed upon a people to keep this promise alive. Only still greater achievements will do it.

The United States is not so strong, the final triumph of the democratic ideal is not so inevitable that we can ignore what the world thinks of us or our record.

Segregation Is Wrong Because It Harms Blacks

Benjamin E. Mays

The most important legal decision ending segregation was *Brown v. Board of Education*, in which the Supreme Court held that segregated schools were inherently unequal and thus unconstitutional. In so ruling, the Court overturned the 1896 judgment in *Plessy v. Ferguson*, which had held that segregation was legal as long as blacks and whites were equally accommodated. Much of the 1954 decision rested on the view that segregation is necessarily unequal because it leads to feelings of inferiority in black school-children. The following article, written shortly after the 1955 Supreme Court ruling that desegregation was to proceed "with all deliberate speed," agrees with the Court's analysis of the harmful effects of segregation. The author, Benjamin E. Mays, argues that segregation is wrong because it harms black people. He also insists that blacks want segregation to end not because they want to mingle with whites but because they want to be able to live with dignity and enjoy the basic services they deserve. Mays also points out that segregation seriously impugns the quality of American democracy in the eyes of the international community. Mays was the son of former slaves, and a major figure in education, religion, and civil rights.

As you read, consider the following questions:
1. Why does the author think discrimination on the basis of race is worse than discrimination on the basis of religion, education, or socio-economic status?

Excerpted from *The Segregation Decisions; Papers Read at a Session of the Twenty-First Annual Meeting of the Southern Historical Association, Memphis, Tennessee, November 10, 1955*, by William Faulkner, Benjamin E. Mays, and Cecil Sims (Atlanta, GA: Southern Regional Council, 1956).

2. Why does Mays think that segregation also harms the segregator, the dominant group that imposes segregation?
3. At the close of his paper, Mays discusses international reaction to segregation. Why, in 1955, was the United States particularly interested in cultivating a positive image of its democracy abroad?

Whenever a strong dominant group possesses all the power, political, educational, economic, and wields all the power; makes all the laws, municipal, state and federal, and administers all the laws; writes all constitutions, municipal, state and federal, and interprets these constitutions; collects and holds all the money, municipal, state, and federal, and distributes all the money; determines all policies—governmental, business, political and educational; when that group plans and places heavy burdens, grievous to be borne, upon the backs of the weak, that act is immoral. If the strong group is a Christian group or a follower of Judaism both of which contend that God is creator, judge, impartial, just, universal, love and that man was created in God's image, the act is against God and man—thus immoral. If the strong group is atheistic, the act is against humanity—still immoral.

No group is wise enough, good enough, strong enough, to assume an omnipotent and omniscient role; no group is good enough, wise enough to restrict the mind, circumscribe the soul, and to limit the physical movements of another group. To do that is blasphemy. It is a usurpation of the role of God.

The Worst Kind of Discrimination

If the strong handicaps the weak on the grounds of race or color, it is all the more immoral because we penalize the group for conditions over which it has no control, for being what nature or nature's God made it. And that is tantamount to saying to God, "You made a mistake, God, when you didn't make all races white." If there were a law which said that an illiterate group had to be segregated, the segregated group could go to school and become literate. If there were a law which said that all peoples with incomes below $5,000 a year had to be segregated, the people under $5,000 a year could strive to rise above the $5,000 bracket. If there were a law which said that men and women who did not bathe had to be segregated, they could develop the habit of daily baths and remove the stigma. If there were a law which said that all groups had to be Catholics, the Jews and Protestants could do something about it by joining the Catholic Church. But to segregate a man because his skin is brown or black, red or yellow, is to segregate a man for circumstances over which he has no control. And of all immoral acts, this is the most immoral.

So the May 17, 1954, Decision of the Supreme Court and all the decisions against segregation are attempts on the part of the judges involved to abolish a great wrong which the strong has deliberately placed upon the backs of the weak. It is an attempt on the part of federal and state judges to remove this stigma, this wrong through constitutional means, which is the democratic, American way.

The Goals of Segregation

I said a moment ago that if the strong deliberately picks out a weak racial group and places upon it heavy burdens that act is immoral. Let me try to analyze this burden, segregation, which has been imposed upon millions of Americans of color. There are at least three main reasons for legal segregation in the United States.

1. The first objective of segregation is to place a legal badge of inferiority upon the segregated, to brand him as unfit to move freely among other human beings. This badge says the segregated is mentally, morally, and socially unfit to move around as a free man.

2. The second objective of segregation is to set the segregated apart so that he can be treated as an inferior: in the courts, in recreation, in transportation, in politics, in government, in employment, in religion, in educa-

tion, in hotels, in motels, restaurants and in every other area of American life. And all of this has been done without the consent of the segregated.

3. The third objective of legalized segregation follows from the first two. It is designed to make the segregated believe that he is inferior, that he is nobody and to make him accept willingly his inferior status in society. It is these conditions which the May 17, 1954, Decision of the Supreme Court and other federal decisions against segregation are designed to correct—to remove this immoral stigma that has been placed upon 16 million Negro Americans, and these are the reasons every thinking Negro wants the legal badge of segregation removed so that he might be able to walk the earth with dignity, as a man, and not cringe and kow-tow as a slave. He believes that this is his God-given right on the earth.

Segregation is immoral because it has inflicted a wound upon the soul of the segregated and so restricted his mind that millions of Negroes now alive will never be cured of the disease of inferiority. Many of them have come to feel and believe that they are inferior or that the cards are so stacked against them that it is useless for them to strive for the highest and the best. Segregate a race for ninety years, tell that race in books, in law, in courts, in education, in church and school, in employment, in transportation, in hotels and motels, in the government that it is inferior—it is bound to leave its damaging mark upon the souls and minds of the segregated. It is these conditions that the federal courts seek to change.

Why Segregation Is Wrong

Any country that restricts the full development of any segment of society retards its own growth and development. The segregated produces less, and even the minds of the strong group are circumscribed because they are often afraid to pursue the whole truth and they spend too much time seeking ways and means of how to keep the segregated group in "its place." Segregation is immoral because it leads to injustice, brutality, and lynching on the part of the group that segregates. The segregated is somebody that can be pushed around as desired by the segregator. As a rule equal justice in the courts is almost impossible for a member of the segregated group if it involves a member of the group imposing segregation. The segregated has no rights that the segregator is bound to respect.

The chief sin of segregation is the distortion of human personality. It damages the soul of both the segregator and the segregated. It gives the segregated a feeling of inherent inferiority which is not based on facts, and it gives the segregator a feeling of superiority which is not based on facts. It is difficult to know who is damaged more—the segregated or the segregator.

It is a false accusation to say that Negroes hail the May 17, 1954, Decision of the Supreme Court because they want to mingle socially with white people. Negroes want segregation abolished because they want the legal stigma of inferiority removed and because they do not believe that equality of educational opportunities can be completely achieved in a society where the law brands a group inferior. When a Negro rides in a Pullman unsegregated he does it not because he wants to ride with white people. He may or may not engage in conversations with a white person. He wants good accommodations. When he eats in an unsegregated diner on the train, he goes in because he is hungry and not because he wants to eat with white people. He goes to the diner not even to mingle with Negroes but to get something to eat. But as he eats and rides he wants no badge of inferiority pinned on his back. He wants to eat and ride with dignity. No Negro clothed in his right mind believes that his social status will be enhanced just because he associates with white people.

Respecting the Law

It is also a false accusation to say that Negroes are insisting that segregated schools must be abolished today or tomor-

Students sit in an overcrowded classroom in Georgia. Some activists argue that segregated schools do not provide black students with an equal education.

row, simultaneously all over the place. As far as I know, no Negro leader has ever advocated that, and they have not even said when desegregation is to be a finished job. They do say that the Supreme Court is the highest law of the land and we should respect that law. Negro leaders do say that each local community should bring together the racial groups in that community, calmly sit down and plan ways and means not how they can circumvent the decision but how they can implement it and plan together when and where they will start. They will be able to start sooner in some places than in others and move faster in some places than in others but begin the process in good faith and with good intent. To deliberately scheme, to deliberately plan through nefarious methods, through violence, boycott and threats to nullify the Decision of the highest law in the land is not only immoral but it encourages a disregard for all laws which we do not like.

We meet the moral issue again. To write into our constitutions things that we do not intend to carry out is an immoral act. I think I am right when I say that most of our states, certainly some of them, say in their constitutions "separate but equal." But you know as well as I do that on the whole the gulf of inequality in education widened with the years. There was no serious attempt nor desire in this country to provide Negroes with educational opportunities equal to those for whites. The great surge to equalize educational opportunities for Negroes did not begin until after 1935 when Murray won his suit to enter the law school of the University of Maryland. It is also clear that the millions poured into Negro education in the last 20 years were appropriated not so much because it was right but in an endeavor to maintain segregation.

We brought this situation upon ourselves. We here in the South have said all along that we believe in segregation but equal segregation. In 1896 in the Louisiana case, *Plessy versus Ferguson*, the United States Supreme Court confirmed the doctrine "separate but equal." But from 1896 to 1935 there was practically nothing done to make the separate equal. When Murray won his case in 1935, we knew we had to move toward equalization. Since 1935 many suits have been won.

It would have been a mighty fine thing if we had obeyed the Supreme Court in 1896 and equalized educational opportunities for Negroes. If we had done that the problem would have been solved because gradually the separate school system would have been abolished and we would have been saved from the agony and fear of this hour. We didn't obey the Supreme Court in 1896 and we do not want to obey it now.

A Decision to Make

Let me say again that the May 17, 1954, Decision of the Supreme Court is an effort to abolish a great evil through orderly processes. And we are morally obligated to implement the Decision or modify the federal constitution and say plainly that this constitution was meant for white people and not for Negroes and that the Declaration of Independence created mostly by the mind of the great southerner, Thomas Jefferson, was meant for white people and not Negroes. Tell the world honestly that we do not believe that part of the Declaration of Independence which says in essence that all men are created equal, that they are endowed by their creator with certain inalienable rights, that among these are life, liberty and the pursuit of happiness.

We are morally obligated to abolish legalized segregation in America or reinterpret the Christian Gospel, the Old and New Testaments, and make the Gospel say that the noble principles of Judaism and Christianity are not applicable to colored peoples and Negroes. Tell the world honestly and plainly that the Fatherhood of God and the Brotherhood of Man cannot work where the colored races are involved. We are morally obligated to move toward implementing the Decision in the deep South or lose our moral leadership in the world. If we do not do it, we must play the role of hypocrisy, preaching one thing and doing another. This is the dilemma which faces our democracy.

The Eyes of the World

The eyes of the world are upon us. One billion or more colored people in Asia and Africa are judging our democracy solely on the basis of how we treat Negroes. White Europe is watching us too. I shall never forget the day in Lucknow, India, when nine reporters from all over India questioned me for 90 minutes about how Negroes are treated in the United States. I shall remember to my dying day the event in 1937 when the principal of an untouchable school introduced me to his boys as an untouchable from the United States [in India, the "untouchables" are lowest in the caste system]. At first it angered me. But on second thought I knew that he was right. Though great progress has been made, for which I am grateful, I and my kind are still untouchables in many sections of the country. There are places where wealth, decency, culture, education, religion, and position will do no good if a Negro. None of these things can take away the mark of untouchability. And the world knows this.

Recently a group of colored students from Asia, Africa,

the Middle East and South America were visiting an outstanding Southern town. All the colored people except those from Africa and Haiti could live in the downtown hotels. The Africans and the Haitians had to seek refuge on the campus of a Negro College. That incident was known to all the other colored students and it will be told many times in Europe, Asia, Africa—and it will not help us in our efforts to democratize the world.

Not long ago a Jew from South Africa and a man from India were guests of a Negro professor. He drove them for several days through the urban and rural sections of his state. The Negro, the host, a citizen of the United States, could not get food from the hotels and restaurants. His guests, one a Jew and the other an Indian, had to go in and buy food for him. The man who introduced me in India as an untouchable was right. The Negro is America's untouchable.

Two or three years ago [the early 1950s] a friend of mine was traveling in Germany. He met a German who had traveled widely in the United States. He told my friend that he hangs his head in shame every time he thinks of what his country did to the Jews—killing six million of them. But he told my friend that after seeing what segregation has done to the soul of the Negro in the South, he has come to the conclusion that it is worse than what Hitler and his colleagues did to the Jews in Germany. He may be wrong but this is what he is telling the people in Germany.

Make no mistake—as this country could not exist half slave and half free, it cannot exist half segregated and half desegregated. The Supreme Court has given America an opportunity to achieve greatness in the area of moral and spiritual things just as it has already achieved greatness in military and industrial might and in material possessions. It is my belief that the South will accept the challenge of the Supreme Court and thus make America and the South safe for democracy.

If we lose this battle for freedom for 15 million Negroes we will lose it for 145 million whites and eventually we will lose it for the world. This is indeed a time for greatness.

Schools Should Be Segregated

James Jackson Kilpatrick

The following selection is drawn from James Jackson Kil-patrick's *The Southern Case for School Segregation*, a 1962 book that argued that schools ought to be segregated on the basis of race. Kilpatrick, who was editor of the *Rich-mond News-Leader*, the most influential daily newspaper in Virginia, from 1951 to 1967, gives his version of life in the South. According to him, for the most part blacks and whites in the South live in harmony. Although boundaries exist, he believes, whites and blacks have more contact with one another in the southern states than they do in the North, where segregation is a matter of fact, if not of law. Kilpatrick argues that there are good reasons to maintain segregation, and in particular he denies, and says that white Southerners overwhelmingly deny, racial equality. According to Kilpatrick, it is patently true that whites as a race are superior, and he insists that white Southerners know this from their own experiences.

As you read, consider the following questions:
1. Of whom is Kilpatrick speaking when he talks of "the South" and "Southerners"?
2. What are Kilpatrick's reasons for thinking race relations in the South are "far closer, more honest, [and] less con-strained" than those in the North?
3. According to Kilpatrick, what is the core reason for op-position to integration?

The best observation to make at the outset is that the South, in general, feels no sharp sense of sin at its "treatment of the Negro." The guilt hypothesis is vastly overdrawn. If wrong has been done (and doubtless wrong has been done), we reflect that within the human relationship wrong always has been done, by one people upon another, since tribal cavemen quarreled with club and stone. And whatever the wrongs may have been, the white South emphatically refuses to accept all the wrongs as her own. For the South itself has been wronged—cruelly and maliciously wronged, by men in high places whose hypocrisy is exceeded only by their ignorance, men whose trade is to damn the bigotry of the segregated South by day and to sleep in lily-white Westchester County by night. We are keenly aware, as Perry Morgan remarked in a telling phrase, of a North that wishes to denounce discrimination and have it too.

But let us begin gently. The Southerner who would grope seriously for understanding of his own perplexing region, and the non-Southerner who would seek in earnest to learn more than his textbooks would tell him, cannot make a start with *Brown* v. *Board of Education* on a May afternoon in 1954. Neither can he begin with *Plessy* v. *Ferguson* in 1896, or with ratification of the Fourteenth Amendment in 1868, or with Appomattox three years earlier. A start has to be made much earlier, in 1619, when the first twenty Negroes arrived from Africa aboard a Dutch slaver and fastened upon the South a wretched incubus that the belated penances of New Englanders have not expiated at all.

A Dual Society
We of the South have been reared from that day in a strange society that only now—and how uncomfortably!—is becoming known at first hand outside the South. This is the dual society, made up of white and Negro coexisting in an oddly intimate remoteness. It is a way of life that has to be experienced. Children mask their eyes and play at being blind. Even so, some of my Northern friends mask their

eyes and play at being Southern; they try to imagine what it must be like to be white in the South, to be Negro in the South. Novelist John Griffin dyed his skin and spent three weeks or so pretending to be Negro, looking for incidents to confirm his prejudices. But a child always knows that he can take his hands from his eyes, and see, that he is not really blind; and those who have not grown up from childhood, and fashioned their whole world from a delicately bounded half a world, cannot comprehend what this is all about. They wash the dye from their imaginations, and put aside *The New York Times*, and awake to a well-ordered society in which the Negroes of their personal acquaintance are sipping martinis and talking of Middle Eastern diplomacy. They form an image of "the Negro" (as men form an image of the French, or the British, or the Japanese) in terms of the slim and elegant Harvard student, the eloquent spokesman of a civil rights group, the trim stenographer in a publishing office: Thurgood Marshall on the bench, Ralph Bunche in the lecture hall. It is a splendid image, finely engraved on brittle glass, an object of universal admiration on the mantle of the *New Republic*. It is an image scarcely known in the South.

A Fact of Life

My father came from New Orleans. His father, a captain in the Confederate Army, returned from the War and established a prosperous business in ship chandlery there. And though I myself was born in Oklahoma, Father having moved there just prior to World War I, we children visited along the Delta in our nonage. We sailed on Pontchartrain, and crabbed at Pass Christian, and once or twice were taken from school in February to sit spellbound on Canal Street and watch the Mardi Gras go by. Our life in Oklahoma was New Orleans once removed; it was a life our playmates accepted as matter-of-factly as children of a coast accept the tides: The Negroes *were;* we *were.* They had their lives; we had ours. There were certain things one did: A proper white child obeyed the family Negroes, ate

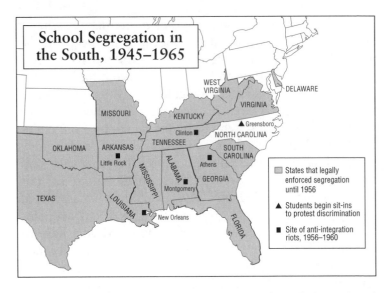

School Segregation in the South, 1945–1965

WEST VIRGINIA
DELAWARE
VIRGINIA
MISSOURI
KENTUCKY
▲ Greensboro
Clinton ■
NORTH CAROLINA
TENNESSEE
OKLAHOMA
ARKANSAS
SOUTH CAROLINA
Little Rock ■
Athens ■
MISSISSIPPI
ALABAMA
GEORGIA
Montgomery ■
TEXAS
LOUISIANA
New Orleans ■
FLORIDA

☐ States that legally enforced segregation until 1956

▲ Students begin sit-ins to protest discrimination

■ Site of anti-integration riots, 1956–1960

with them, bothered them, teased them, loved them, lived with them, learned from them. And there were certain things one did not do: One did not intrude upon their lives, or ask about Negro institutions, or bring a Negro child in the front door. And at five, or six, or seven, one accepted, without question, that Calline and Cubboo, who were vaguely the charges of a Negro gardener up the street, had their schools; and we had ours.

Does all this have the air of a chapter from William Gilmore Simms or a post-bellum romance by Thomas Nelson Page? I myself lived it, forty years ago; my own sons have lived it in this generation. My father lived it, and his father before him. For three hundred years, the South has lived with this subconsciousness of race. Who hears a clock tick, or the surf murmur, or the trains pass? Not those who live by the clock or the sea or the track. In the South, the acceptance of racial separation begins in the cradle. What rational man imagines this concept can be shattered overnight?

We had two Negroes who served my family more than twenty years. One was Lizzie. The other was Nash. Lizzie was short and plump and placid, and chocolate-brown; she "lived on," in a room and bath over the garage, and her broad face never altered in its kindness. Nash was short and slim, older, better educated, more a leader; she was African-black; and as a laundress, she came in after church on Sundays, put the clothes down to soak in the basement tubs, gossiped with Lizzie, scolded her, raised Lizzie's sights. On Monday, the two of them did the wash, hanging the clothes on heavy wire lines outside the kitchen door, and late in the afternoon Nash ironed. She pushed the iron with an economical push-push, thump; turn the shirt; push-push, thump. And I would come home from school to the smell of starch and the faint scorch of the iron and the push-push, thump, and would descend to the basement only to be ordered upstairs to wash my hands and change out of school clothes.

Toward the end of their lives, disaster came to both of them. Lizzie went slowly blind, through some affliction no surgeon could correct, and Nash lost the middle three fingers of one hand when her scarf tangled in the bellows of a church organ. Nevertheless, they stayed with us until age at last put them on the sidelines. And as far as love and devotion and respect can reach, they were members of the family. Yet I often have wondered, in later years, did we children know them? Did Mother and Father know them? I do not think we did.

A Unique Relationship

This relationship, loving but unknowing, has characterized the lives of thousands of Southern children on farms and in the cities too. White infants learn to feel invisible fences as they crawl, to sense unwritten boundaries as they walk. And I know this much, that Negro children are brought up to sense these boundaries too. What is so often misunderstood, outside the South, is this delicate intimacy of human beings whose lives are so intricately bound together. I have met Northerners who believe, in all apparent seriousness, that segregation in the South means literally that: *segregation*, the races stiffly apart, never touching. A wayfaring stranger from the New York *Herald Tribune* implied as much in a piece he wrote from Virginia after the school decision. His notion was that whites and Negroes did not even say "good morning" to each other. God in heaven!

In plain fact, the relationship between white and Negro in the segregated South, in the country and in the city, has been far closer, more honest, less constrained, than such relations generally have been in the integrated North. In Charleston and New Orleans, among many other cities, residential segregation does not exist, for example, as it exists in Detroit or Chicago. In the country, whites and Negroes are farm neighbors. They share the same calamities —the mud, the hail, the weevils—and they minister, in their own unfelt, unspoken way, to one another. Is the relationship that of master and servant, superior and inferior? Down deep, doubtless it is, but I often wonder if this is more of a wrong to the Negro than the affected, hearty "equality" encountered in the North. . . .

A Shift in Reasons

I say this relationship "has been," and in the past perfect lies a melancholy change that disturbs many Southerners deeply. In my observation, a tendency grows in much of the white South to acknowledge and to abandon, with no more than a ritual protest, many of the patent absurdities of "Jim Crow." Many of these practices, so deeply resented in recent years by the Negro, may have had some rational basis when they were instituted in the post-Reconstruction period. When the first trolleys came along, the few Negroes who rode them were mostly servants; others carried with them the fragrance of farm or livery stable. A Jim Crow section perhaps made sense in those days. But in my own nonage, during the 1920s, and in the years since then, few Southerners ever paused to examine the reasons for segregation on streetcars. We simply moved the little portable sign that separated white from Negro as a car filled up, and whites sat in front of the sign and Negroes sat behind it. This was the way we rode streetcars. After *Brown* v. *Board of Education*, when the abiding subconsciousness of the Negro turned overnight into an acute and immediate awareness of the Negro, some of these laws and customs ceased to be subject to reason anyhow; they became, confusingly, matters of strategy; they became occupied ground in an undeclared war, not to be yielded lest their yielding be regarded as needless surrender. Many aspects of our lives have gone that way since. The unwritten rules of generations are now being, in truth, unwritten; in their place, it is proposed by the apostles of instant integration that there be no rules at all. It seems so easy: "What difference does the color of a man's skin make?" "Why not just treat them as equals?" "There is no such thing as race."

Ah, but it is not so easy. The ingrained attitudes of a lifetime cannot be jerked out like a pair of infected molars, and new porcelain dentures put in their place. For this is what our Northern friends will not comprehend: The South, agreeable as it may be to confessing some of its sins and to bewailing its more manifest wickednesses, simply does not concede that at bottom its basic attitude is "infected" or wrong. On the contrary, the Southerner rebelliously clings to what seems to him the hard core of truth in this whole controversy: *Here and now*, in his own communities, in the mid-1960s, the Negro race, as a race, plainly is not equal to the white race, as a race; nor, for that matter, in the wider world beyond, by the accepted judgment of ten thousand years, has the Negro race, as a race, *ever* been the cultural or intellectual equal of the white race, as a race.

A Dissenting View

This we take to be a plain statement of fact, and if we are not amazed that our Northern antagonists do not accept it as such, we are resentful that they will not even look at the proposition, or hear of it, or inquire into it. Those of us who have ventured to discuss the issues outside the South have discovered, whenever the point arises, that no one is so intolerant of truth as academicians whose profession it is to pursue it. The whole question of race has become a closed question: the earth is a cube, and there's an end to it; Two and two are four, the sun rises in the east, and no race is inferior to any other race. Even the possibility of a conflicting hypothesis is beyond the realm of sober examination. John Hope Franklin, chairman of the history department at Brooklyn College, sees Southern attitudes on race as a "hoax." Their wrongness is "indisputable." To Ashley Montagu, race is a myth. A UNESCO pamphlet makes the flat, unqualified statement that "modern biological and psychological studies of the differences between races do not support the idea that one is superior to another as far as innate potentialities are concerned." And when one inquires, why, pray, has it taken so long for the Negro's innately equal potentialities to emerge, the answers trail off into lamentations on the conditions under which the Negro has lived. Thus, the doctrine of environment, like the principle of charity, is trotted out to conceal a multitude of sins. The fault, if there be any fault, is held to be not in men's genes, but in their substandard housing.

All this is to anticipate some of the points this brief is intended to develop, but it is perhaps as well to know where the argument is going. The South does not wish to be cruel, or unkind, or intolerant, or bigoted; but in this area it does not wish to be unrealistic either. We do not agree that our "prejudice" in this regard is prejudice at all, in the pejorative sense in which the word is widely used. The man who wakes up ten times with a hangover, having had too much brandy the night before, is not "prejudiced" against brandy if on the eleventh occasion he passes the brandy by; he has merely learned to respect its qualities. And what others see as the dark night of our bigotry is regarded, in our own observation, as the revealing light of experience.

Change in the South Is Inevitable

Lenoir Chambers

In the following piece, Lenoir Chambers reflects on the changes he sees his native South facing after the landmark Supreme Court decision in *Brown v. Board of Education.* However unwelcome that decision may be, Chambers argues, Southerners must be prepared to accept the ruling, and he discusses and rejects several arguments which aim to undermine the legitimacy of the Court's finding. In particular, he denies that the Supreme Court ruling was the work of Chief Justice Earl Warren alone, and argues that the ruling's unanimity is a sure sign that the law is clear. For Chambers, white Southerners have to face the fact that their unifying principle, that the South belongs to white people, is no longer tenable. The political, educational, and economic maturity of blacks, he argues, as well as general national trends and influence, mark an era of historic transition that cannot be avoided. Furthermore, he concludes, the forces that make change inevitable are not uniquely American, but are at work throughout the world, in other places where people seek independence and dignity. Chambers was editor of the *Norfolk Virginia-Pilot* and, although not in favor of integration, spoke out against the illogical and emotional arguments many newspapers in the South used against desegregation.

As you read, consider the following questions:
1. Why might Chambers feel the need to defend the Supreme Court's ruling?

Excerpted from "The Great Opportunity," by Lenoir Chambers in *We Dissent*, edited by Hoke Norris (New York: St. Martin's Press, 1962). Copyright © 1962 by Lenoir Chambers. Reprinted with permission.

2. What arguments does Chambers offer for thinking that change in the South is inevitable?
3. In what ways does Chambers think that the black community in the South has changed?

The decisive fact confronting the Southern States in May of 1954 and again in May of 1955 was that the Supreme Court, in effect, had convicted them of unconstitutional discrimination in the operation of their public school systems. It had directed them to change these racial practices.

This is an awkward position for States to be caught in. Although the turbulence of the succeeding years has made many men forget it, the Supreme Court was aware of the problems and difficulties in changes of great social depth—even if it did not possess the genius to foresee all of them—that compliance with its decisions would entail. In its hearings of the cases embodied in *Brown v. Board of Education,* the court invited the participation of the attorney general of the United States and the attorneys general of other States besides those involved directly in the litigation. It posed questions which it said it would like to have answered for its guidance. It separated the decision in principle (1954) and the decision as to compliance (1955) by a full year in order that the nature of the changes might sink in and that all people—perhaps starting with the court itself—might have time to think about what should come next.

Before arriving at the decision as to compliance, the court again invited answers to questions about specific lines of action on which it desired advice. After arriving at the decision as to compliance, the Supreme Court directed the district courts to make arrangements in accordance with conditions that varied from State to State. (There are many Souths.) It is a rare issue that discloses the Supreme Court showing so much concern about how to give reality to what it had concluded the Constitution required.

This judicial concern could not lessen materially the formidable extent of the Southern embarrassment. Everyone knew that deep changes were in progress in Southern life. But the public assumptions and the political commitments still prevailing in many parts of the South had not advanced far beyond Ulrich Bonnell Phillips' definition of the unifying principle and central theme of Southern history: that the South "shall be and remain a white man's country."

Yet here was the Supreme Court saying in its 1954 decision that "in the field of public education the doctrine of 'separate but equal' has no place" because "separate educational facilities are inherently unequal." And here was the court saying in its 1955 decision that "the [Federal] courts will require that the defendants make a prompt and reasonable start toward full compliance" with the 1954 ruling.

The Supreme Court had arrived at these conclusions by unanimous votes. Justice Harlan succeeded Justice Jackson between the 1954 and 1955 decisions, and the total for the two decisions is ten justices. Three other justices who have taken their seats on the court since May, 1955, have participated in subsequent decisions growing out of the two basic decisions, with no indication of unhappiness over the court's record. In all, then, thirteen Supreme Court justices made the original decisions, or accepted them, or amplified them in detail. None has ever dissented.

It is still the fashion in some quarters to attribute these decisions and this unanimity to the influence of Chief Justice Warren. Those who say "the Warren court" rarely smile when they say it. But this is plainly a political interpretation, not based in its derogatory intent on fact or reasoning.

Chief Justice Warren took his seat on the court on October 3, 1953. When he read the decision in *Brown v. Board of Education* on May 17, 1954, he had been a member of the court for seven and a half months. Earlier he had been a State attorney general, a governor, and a candidate for vice president. He was not without public influence. But the Supreme Court had been considering these cases since 1952. It had made decisions in higher education cases that pointed in the same direction. Its justices are perennially characterized by independence, individualism, depth of conviction, pride of opinion, and even touches of prima donna-ism. Over the decades the court may tend to follow the election returns, as the Dooley dictum postulated, but any supposition that it scrambles into line behind the chief justice—*any* chief justice—has no evidence to support it.

More specifically, you engage in pure fantasy if you suppose that Earl Warren could pull around by the nose Hugo Black, Stanley F. Reed, Felix Frankfurter, William O. Douglas, Robert H. Jackson, Harold H. Burton, Tom C. Clark, Sherman Minton, and John Marshall Harlan, and in later years William J. Brennan, Jr., Charles E. Whittaker, and Potter Stewart. If there was a case against the decisions, it would have to rest on something more substantial than tall talk about the chief justice's machinations or his personal or official dominance over the brains and backbones of his associates.

Was there anything more substantial in the objections to the ruling? The list of allegations is long: The Supreme Court had no jurisdiction in educational matters. The court had already settled the segregation issue in *Plessy v. Ferguson* (1896), the "separate but equal" doctrine of which later was extended to school situations. The court had no "right" to reverse this decision fifty-eight years later. When the court rested its decision on the Fourteenth Amendment it relied on an amendment that had not been ratified constitutionally and ought now to be wrenched out of the Constitution. The court had produced no constitutional basis or reasoning for a judgment that "separate educational facilities are inherently unequal." The court had proclaimed its lack of legal justification when it cited social philosophers in a footnote, especially Gunnar Myrdal, who had written some uncomplimentary judgments about Southern institutions and about the Constitution itself. And so on.

Most of these attacks plainly lack the force of fact or logic. If the Constitution does not speak specifically of education, it declares specifically that "no state shall make or enforce *any law* which shall abridge the privileges or immunities of citizens of the United States . . . *nor deny to any person* within its jurisdiction the equal protection of the laws." (The italics are supplied.) That broad limitation on the States has often been held to be of sufficient authority for the courts to prohibit State action of many kinds. Clearly the States cannot step over such limits without inviting judicial rebuke.

Nor can protesters grant jurisdiction to the Supreme Court in *Plessy v. Ferguson,* thereby accepting the court's authority to lay down the "separate but equal" doctrine, without granting to the court jurisdiction in a case brought to overturn the doctrine of "separate but equal." If the court could consider the one, it could consider the other.

Nor is it possible to ignore the fact that the Supreme Court has been reversing itself cheerfully from far back in its history, often with the approval of revered exemplars of judicial wisdom among its members. In two cases, one in 1932 and the other in 1944, the court itself counted forty overrulings that it had made of earlier decisions.

An academic argument might be made about the manner in which the Fourteenth Amendment was ratified. But that amendment had stood up for eighty-six years (ninety-four years now), and the 1960's are a little late for overturning the American Civil War of the 1860's. People who argue Calhoun in the age of Kennedy do so, necessarily, in the spirit of those who debate what would have happened at Gettysburg if Stonewall Jackson had been there. The issue has its points as a conversation piece, but it does not have much reality.

The substance of the constitutional argument in the 1954 decision, the heart of the question of whether separate educational facilities in the public schools create unconstitutional discrimination, can be argued a long time and no doubt will be. But it will be argued, I think, with less and less conviction as more and more of the old lines of segregation in Southern life are worn thin from much crossing over and prove difficult to trace, and eventually are obliterated altogether. . . .

The South stands in an era of historic transition that began long before the Supreme Court decisions of 1954 and 1955. It is the era of the coming of age of the American Negro citizenship, politically and economically; and it is proclaiming itself in all aspects of life in the South. There is no possible way of averting this transition. If no other influences assure its continuation, education would. The Southern States cannot send hundreds of thousands of Negro boys and girls to public schools every year, and tens of thousands of Negro young people to colleges and universities, without expecting, when university, college, or even high school courses are completed, that an increasing number of them will rise up and look around and ask, "Where do we stand in the scheme of things?"

Education alone would do it, but other influences pressing to the same end are numerous and powerful. They include all the means of communication, old and new; the national business and commercial operations that have no regard for sections, regions, or State borders, or for race, color, or creed; the lessons of war and the desegregation of the armed forces; the requirements of international leadership; the shifting tides of population; the achievements of Negroes in the arts and in sports; the objectivity of modern historians and the minds of modern writers.

Even influences that flow out of the life of America are not all. For the coming of age of the Negro citizenship of the United States coincides with the coming of independence and the rise of many new peoples around the globe. Their color, often dark, and their background as they have surged upward to seek national dignity, have had their influence on the thinking of American Negroes. The differences are deep and numerous, but the world movement and the movement within the United States (which has relied on American constitutional methods only) have not only come in the same era: they have reflected a spirit that is alive and vibrant in the world today. It would be remarkable if the one did not affect the other.

CHAPTER

2

THE ROLE OF GOVERNMENT

CHAPTER PREFACE

Although the push for desegregation was in many ways about the hearts and minds of people, it had much to do with government. Indeed, particularly in the southern states, segregation was enforced by law as much as by social custom. Furthermore, when the Supreme Court in *Brown v. Board of Education* rejected segregated schools as unconstitutional, state governments in the South responded with the policies of interposition and massive resistance, according to which they would use all legal means to avoid desegregation. In addition, local police forces were often more interested in preserving racial segregation than they were the law of the land. The federal government, especially the executive branch, played a key role in ending segregation, and struggles between federal, state, and local governments were as common as those between private citizens.

One of the key areas of conflict was whether the legality of segregation was a federal or a state issue. The Supreme Court, in ruling that segregated schools violated the Fourteenth Amendment to the U.S. Constitution, clearly was of the opinion that segregation was a federal matter given that the Constitution applies to all citizens in whichever state they may be. In 1956, however, shortly after the Supreme Court's *Brown v. Board of Education* ruling, one hundred congressmen from the South signed a declaration announcing their intention to resist implementing the Court's finding. As they saw it, the judgment violated the Constitution by interfering with the rights of states to determine education policy. For these congressmen, whether schools were to be segregated was an issue that states should decide, and they vigorously objected to what they saw as federal interference. Others, such as the editorial writer at the *Arkansas Gazette,* believed that state governments, by resisting integration, were interfering in what should have been a local process, conducted at the level of the school boards.

Some of the most dramatic moments in the civil rights movement occurred when federal troops, under the command of the president, ensured successful desegregation at southern schools. In 1957, for instance, Arkansas governor Orval Faubus, ostensibly to preserve the peace, ordered Arkansas National Guardsmen to surround Little Rock Central High School, which was to admit its first black students. Eventually, when it became clear that Faubus had no intention of allowing the school to be integrated, President Dwight D. Eisenhower placed the troops under federal command and allowed integration to proceed. In explaining his actions to the nation, Eisenhower focused on law and order, and insisted that the federal government had an obligation to enforce federal law when state and local authorities refused to do so. A quite different line of argument was advanced several years later by President John F. Kennedy when he ordered the Alabama National Guard, again against the orders of the state governor, to ensure the successful integration of the University of Alabama. In his national address, Kennedy argued that segregation was a moral wrong demanding the attention of the whole country. Because tensions between state and federal governments were often high, many saw the federal government as a strong defender of civil rights. To others, though, the actions of the federal government were largely cosmetic, and they pointed with concern to the numerous instances in which the federal government refused to intervene.

The Supreme Court Judgment Violates the Constitution

Walter F. George et al.

The Supreme Court's 1954 decision in *Brown v. Board of Education*, which ruled that segregated schools violated the Fourteenth Amendment, which guarantees citizens equal protection of the law, shocked and outraged many white Southerners. In March 1956, nineteen senators and eighty-one representatives from the South signed a declaration, which was then read into the *Congressional Record*. In that declaration, which has come to be known as the Southern Manifesto, the members of Congress declare the Supreme Court's ruling in *Brown v. Board of Education* unconstitutional. Specifically, the congressmen argue that the intention behind the Fourteenth Amendment was never to ban "separate but equal" facilities, and they reproach the Supreme Court for what they see as unwarranted interference with the Constitution and with the rights of states to determine education policy. Walter F. George, a principal author of the Manifesto and its presenter, served as a senator in Georgia from 1922 until 1957.

As you read, consider the following questions:
1. Why do the signers of the Southern Manifesto think that the Fourteenth Amendment should not be interpreted to bar segregated schools?
2. How do the signers of the declaration characterize the relationship between blacks and whites in the South?

Excerpted from the *United States of America Congressional Record: Proceedings and Debates of the 84th Congress, Second Session*, by the U.S. Congress (Washington, DC: U.S. Government Printing Office, 1956).

3. Does legal segregation, as the signers of the Manifesto argue, respect the right of parents to "direct the lives and education of their own children"?

Declaration of Constitutional Principles
The unwarranted decision of the Supreme Court in the public school cases is now bearing the fruit always produced when men substitute naked power for established law.

The Founding Fathers gave us a Constitution of checks and balances because they realized the inescapable lesson of history that no man or group of men can be safely entrusted with unlimited power. They framed this Constitution with its provisions for change by amendment in order to secure the fundamentals of government against the dangers of temporary popular passion or the personal predilections of public officeholders.

We regard the decision of the Supreme Court in the school cases as a clear abuse of judicial power. It climaxes a trend in the Federal Judiciary undertaking to legislate, in derogation of the authority of Congress, and to encroach upon the reserved rights of the States and the people.

The original Constitution does not mention education. Neither does the 14th amendment nor any other amendment. The debates preceding the submission of the 14th amendment clearly show that there was no intent that it should affect the system of education maintained by the States.

Segregation Not Unconstitutional

The very Congress which proposed the amendment subsequently provided for segregated schools in the District of Columbia.

When the amendment was adopted in 1868, there were 37 States of the Union. . . .

Every one of the 26 States that had any substantial racial differences among its people, either approved the operation of segregated schools already in existence or subsequently established such schools by action of the same law-making body which considered the 14th amendment.

As admitted by the Supreme Court in the public school case (*Brown* v. *Board of Education*), the doctrine of separate but equal schools "apparently originated in *Roberts* v. *City of Boston* (1849), upholding school segregation against attack as being violative of a State constitutional guarantee of equality." This constitutional doctrine began in the North, not in the South, and it was followed not only in Massachusetts, but in Connecticut, New York, Illinois, Indiana, Michigan, Minnesota, New Jersey, Ohio, Pennsylvania and other northern States until they, exercising their rights as States through the constitutional processes of local self-government, changed their school systems.

In the case of *Plessy* v. *Ferguson* in 1896 the Supreme Court expressly declared that under the 14th amendment no person was denied any of his rights if the States provided separate but equal public facilities. This decision has been followed in many other cases. It is notable that the Supreme Court, speaking through Chief Justice Taft, a former President of the United States, unanimously declared in 1927 in *Lum* v. *Rice* that the "separate but equal" principle is "within the discretion of the State in regulating its public schools and does not conflict with the 14th amendment."

A Way of Life
This interpretation, restated time and again, became a part of the life of the people of many of the States and confirmed their habits, customs, traditions, and way of life. It is founded on elemental humanity and commonsense, for parents should not be deprived by Government of the right to direct the lives and education of their own children.

Though there has been no constitutional amendment or act of Congress changing this established legal principle almost a century old, the Supreme Court of the United States, with no legal basis for such action, undertook to exercise their naked judicial power and substituted their personal political and social ideas for the established law of the land.

This unwarranted exercise of power by the Court, contrary to the Constitution, is creating chaos and confusion in the States principally affected. It is destroying the amicable relations between the white and Negro races that have been created through 90 years of patient effort by the good people of both races. It has planted hatred and suspicion where there has been heretofore friendship and understanding.

Without regard to the consent of the governed, outside agitators are threatening immediate and revolutionary changes in our public-school systems. If done, this is certain to destroy the system of public education in some of the States.

A Pledge to Resist

With the gravest concern for the explosive and dangerous condition created by this decision and inflamed by outside meddlers:

We reaffirm our reliance on the Constitution as the fundamental law of the land.

We decry the Supreme Court's encroachments on rights reserved to the States and to the people, contrary to established law, and to the Constitution.

We commend the motives of those States which have declared the intention to resist forced integration by any lawful means.

We appeal to the States and people who are not directly affected by these decisions to consider the constitutional principles involved against the time when they too, on issues vital to them, may be the victims of judicial encroachment.

Even though we constitute a minority in the present Congress, we have full faith that a majority of the American people believe in the dual system of government which has enabled us to achieve our greatness and will in time demand that the reserved rights of the States and of the people be made secure against judicial usurpation.

We pledge ourselves to use all lawful means to bring about a reversal of this decision which is contrary to the

Constitution and to prevent the use of force in its implementation.

In this trying period, as we all seek to right this wrong, we appeal to our people not to be provoked by the agitators and troublemakers invading our States and to scrupulously refrain from disorder and lawless acts.

States Have a Right to Preserve Segregation

George C. Wallace

After George C. Wallace lost to John Patterson in the 1958 race to become governor of Alabama, he vowed to never again be outdone as an advocate of segregation. Patterson's victory was in large measure due to his stronger record on defending racial discrimination and the greater emphasis he placed on maintaining segregation in his advertisements and speeches. In the 1962 election campaign, Wallace kept his promise to himself, and on January 14, 1963, he delivered his inaugural address as governor, pledging "Segregation today, segregation tomorrow, segregation forever." In this speech, reprinted below, Wallace casts the issue of segregation as an issue of state's rights, and he insists that the federal government's efforts to desegregate the South infringe the liberty of the citizens of Alabama. In Wallace's opinion, different races should live separately, and he sees the battle against desegregation as divinely inspired by God. In the decade following his election, Wallace relentlessly opposed federal efforts to desegregate schools and to end widespread voting discrimination practices.

As you read, consider the following questions:
1. Whom is Wallace talking about when he uses the words "We," "Our," and "Us"?
2. Wallace says the fight to preserve segregation is a fight to preserve "freedoms and liberties." What arguments does he offer in support of this view?
3. According to Wallace, the fight against desegregation is a divine mission, backed by God. How does Wallace char-

Excerpted from George C. Wallace's inaugural address, Montgomery, Alabama, January 14, 1963.

acterize the federal government, and what does he think inspires the desire for a strong federal government?

This is the day of my Inauguration as Governor of the State of Alabama. And on this day I feel a deep obligation to renew my pledges, my covenants with you, the people of this great state. General Robert E. Lee said that "duty" is the sublimest word in the English language and I have come, increasingly, to realize what he meant. I shall do my duty to you, God helping, to every man, to every woman, yes, to every child in this state. I shall fulfill my duty toward honesty and economy in our State government so that no man shall have a part of his livelihood cheated and no child shall have a bit of his future stolen away. . . .

Today I have stood, where once Jefferson Davis stood, and took an oath to my people. It is very appropriate then that from this Cradle of the Confederacy, this very Heart of the Great Anglo-Saxon Southland, that today we sound the drum for freedom as have our generations of forebears before us done, time and time again through history. Let us rise to the call of freedom-loving blood that is in us and send our answer to the tyranny that clanks its chains upon the South. In the name of the greatest people that have ever trod this earth, I draw the line in the dust and toss the gauntlet before the feet of tyranny and I say: segregation today, segregation tomorrow, segregation forever.

The Washington, D.C., school riot report is disgusting and revealing. We will not sacrifice our children to any such type school system—and you can write that down. The federal troops in Mississippi could be better used guarding the safety of the citizens of Washington, D.C., where it is even unsafe to walk or go to a ballgame—and that is the nation's capitol. I was safer in a B-29 bomber over Japan during the war in an air raid, than the people of Washington are walking to the White House neighborhood. A closer example is Atlanta. The city officials fawn for political reasons over school integration and Then build barricades to stop residential integration—what hypocrisy!

Let us send this message back to Washington by our representatives who are with us today: that from this day we are standing up, and the heel of tyranny does not fit the neck of an upright man; that we intend to take the offensive and carry our fight for freedom across the nation, wielding the balance of power we know we possess in the Southland; that we, not the insipid bloc of voters of some sections, will determine in the next election who shall sit in the White House of these United States; that from this day, from this hour, from this minute, we give the word of a race of honor that we will tolerate their boot in our face no longer. And let those certain judges put *that* in their opium pipes of power and smoke it for what it is worth.

Hear me, Southerners! You sons and daughters who have moved north and west throughout this nation, we call on you from your native soil to join with us in national support and vote, and we know, wherever you are, away from the hearths of the Southland, that you will respond, for though you may live in the fartherest reaches of this vast country, your heart has never left Dixieland.

And you native sons and daughters of old New England's rock-ribbed patriotism, and you sturdy natives of the great Mid-West, and you descendants of the far West flaming spirit of pioneer freedom, we invite you to come and be with us, for you are of the Southern spirit and the Southern philosophy. You are Southerners too and brothers with us in our fight. . . .

The Threat of Government

We are faced with an idea that if a centralized government assumes enough authority, enough power over its people, that it can provide a utopian life. That [it,] if given the power to dictate, to forbid, to require, to demand, to distribute, to edict and to judge what is best and enforce that, will produce only "good," and it shall be our father and our God. It is an idea of government that encourages our fears and destroys our faith, for where there is faith, there is no fear, and where there is fear, there is no faith. . . .

We find we have replaced faith with fear, and though we may give lip service to the Almighty, in reality, government has become our god. It is, therefore, a basically ungodly government and its appeal to the pseudo-intellectual and the politician is to change their status from servant of the people to master of the people, to play at being God without faith in God and without the wisdom of God. It is a system that is the very opposite of Christ for it feeds and encourages everything degenerate and base in our people as it assumes the responsibilities that we ourselves should assume. Its pseudo-liberal spokesmen and some Harvard advocates have never examined the logic of its substitution of what it calls "human rights" for individual rights, for its propaganda play on words has appeal for the unthinking. Its logic is totally material and irresponsible as it runs the full gamut of human desires, including the theory that everyone has voting rights without the spiritual responsibility of preserving freedom. Our founding fathers recognized those rights, but only within the framework of those spiritual responsibilities. But the strong, simple faith and sane reasoning of our founding fathers have long since been forgotten as the so-called "progressives" tell us that our Constitution was written for "horse and buggy" days. So were the Ten Commandments. . . .

To Live and Work Apart

This nation was never meant to be a unit of one, but a united of the many. That is the exact reason our freedom loving forefathers established the states, so as to divide the rights and powers among the states, insuring that no central power could gain master government control.

In united effort we were meant to live under this government, whether Baptist, Methodist, Presbyterian, Church of Christ, or whatever one's denomination or religious belief, each respecting the others' right to a separate denomination, each, by working to develop his own, enriching the total of all our lives through united effort. And so it was meant in our political lives, whether Republican, Democrat, Prohibition, or whatever political party, each striving from his separate political station, respecting the rights of others to be separate and work from within their political framework, and each separate political station making its contribution to our lives.

And so it was meant in our racial lives, each race, within its own framework has the freedom to teach, to instruct, to develop, to ask for and receive deserved help from others of separate racial stations. This is the great freedom of our American founding fathers, but if we amalgamate into the one unit as advocated by the communist philosophers, then the enrichment of our lives, the freedom for our development, is gone forever. We become, therefore, a mongrel unit of one under a single all powerful government and we stand for everything and for nothing. . . .

The true brotherhood of America, of respecting the separateness of others and uniting in effort, has been so twisted and distorted from its original concept that there is a small wonder that communism is winning the world.

We invite the negro citizens of Alabama to work with us from his separate racial station, as we will work with him, to develop, to grow in individual freedom and enrichment. We want jobs and a good future for both races, the tubercular and the infirm. This is the basic heritage of my religion, of which I make full practice, for we are all the handiwork of God.

But we warn those, of any group, who would follow the false doctrine of communistic amalgamation that we will not surrender our system of government, our freedom of race and religion, that freedom was won at a hard price and if it requires a hard price to retain it, we are able and quite willing to pay it. . . .

Southerners and Freedom
We remind all within hearing of this Southland that a *Southerner*, Peyton Randolph, presided over the Continen-

tal Congress in our nation's beginning, that a *Southerner*, Thomas Jefferson, wrote the Declaration of Independence, that a *Southerner*, George Washington, is the Father of our country, that a *Southerner*, James Madison, authored our Constitution, that a *Southerner*, George Mason, authored the Bill of Rights and it was a Southerner who said, "Give me liberty or give me death," Patrick Henry.

Southerners played a most magnificent part in erecting this great divinely inspired system of freedom and as God is our witness, Southerners will save it.

Let us, as Alabamians, grasp the hand of destiny and walk out of the shadow of fear and fill our divine destination. Let us not simply defend, but let us assume the leadership of the fight and carry our leadership across this nation. God has placed us here in this crisis. Let us not fail in this, our most historical moment.

You are here today, present in this audience, and to you over this great state, wherever you are in sound of my voice, I want to humbly and with all sincerity, thank you for your faith in me.

I promise you that I will try to make you a good governor. I promise you that, as God gives me the wisdom and the strength, I will be sincere with you. I will be honest with you.

I will apply the old sound rule of our fathers, that anything worthy of our defense is worthy of one hundred percent of our defense. I have been taught that freedom meant freedom from any threat or fear of government. I was born in that freedom, I was raised in that freedom. I intend to live life in that freedom and God willing, when I die, I shall leave that freedom to my children, as my father left it to me.

My pledge to you, to "Stand up for Alabama," is a stronger pledge today than it was the first day I made that pledge. I shall "Stand up for Alabama," as Governor of our State. You stand with me and we, together, can give courageous leadership to millions of people throughout this nation who look to the South for their hope in this fight to win and preserve our freedoms and liberties.

States Should Stay Out of Local Integration Efforts

Arkansas Gazette

In early September 1957, a small group of black students was to begin attending the previously all-white Central High School in Little Rock, Arkansas. The day before the nine students were to enter Central High, however, Governor Orval Faubus ordered National Guardsmen to surround the school. He took this unusual action, he explained in a televised speech later that night, because he had heard reports of impending violence between white supremacists and black residents. Faubus ordered blacks to stay away from Central High and whites to stay away from Horace Mann, the black high school, and he declared that if black students tried to enter Central High, "blood would run in the streets." The following editorial, published in the *Arkansas Gazette* on September 4, expresses suspicion concerning the motives of Governor Faubus and argues that the blame for the crisis rests squarely upon his shoulders. In the eyes of the *Gazette*, the issue is no longer about racial integration alone but is also about whether the rulings and decisions of U.S. courts will be ignored by state officials.

As you read, consider the following questions:
1. In the eyes of the editorial writer, what level of government should be dealing with the integration of students in Little Rock, Arkansas?
2. What does the editorial suggest is the real reason Governor Faubus called in the National Guard?
3. The editorial argues that Governor Faubus is creating a problem rather than responding to an already existing

problem. What reasons are offered for thinking this is correct?

Little Rock arose yesterday to gaze upon the incredible spectacle of an empty high school surrounded by National Guard troops called out by Governor Faubus to protect life and property against a mob that never materialized.

Mr. Faubus says he based this extraordinary action on reports of impending violence. Dozens of local reporters and national correspondents worked through the day yesterday without verifying the few facts the governor offered to explain why his appraisal was so different from that of local officials—who have asked for no such action.

Mr. Faubus contends that he has done nothing that can be construed as defiance of the federal government.

Federal Judge Ronald N. Davies last night accepted the governor's statement at its face value, and ordered the School Board to proceed on the assumption that the National Guard would protect the right of the nine enrolled Negro children to enter high school without interference.

Now it remains for Mr. Faubus to decide whether he intends to pose what could be the most serious constitutional question to face the national government since the Civil War. The effect of his action so far is to interpose his state office between the local School District and the United States Court. The government, as Judge Davies implied last night, now has no choice but to proceed against such interference or abandon its right to enforce its rulings and decisions.

Making the Problem Bigger

Thus the issue is no longer segregation vs. integration. The question has now become the supremacy of the government of the United States in all matters of law. And clearly the federal government cannot let this issue remain unsolved, no matter what the cost to this community.

Until last Thursday the matter of gradual, limited integration in the Little Rock schools was a local problem which had been well and wisely handled by responsible local officials who have had—and we believe still have—the support of a majority of the people of this city. On that day Mr. Faubus appeared in Chancery Court on behalf of a small but militant minority and chose to make it a state problem. On Monday night he called out the National Guard and made it a national problem.

It is one he must now live with, and the rest of us must suffer under. If Mr. Faubus in fact has no intention of defying federal authority now is the time for him to call a halt to the resistance which is preventing the carrying out of a duly entered court order. And certainly he should do so before his own actions become the cause of the violence he professes to fear.

Citizens Must Obey the Laws

Dwight D. Eisenhower

Desegregation was scheduled to begin in early September 1957, at Little Rock Central High School in Arkansas. The day before nine black students were to begin attending, however, the state governor, Orval Faubus, ordered National Guardsmen to surround the school and keep the black students out, ostensibly in order to protect them from angry white supremacists. Three weeks later the situation was still not resolved, and to most observers it was clear that local and state authorities were deliberately thwarting federal law, whatever they may have claimed to the contrary. On September 24, President Dwight D. Eisenhower issued an executive order that authorized the use of federal troops to ensure the black students were able to attend safely, and that evening he addressed the nation. In his speech, reprinted below, Eisenhower insists that the federal government has a duty to enforce federal law when local and state authorities fail to do so.

As you read, consider the following questions:
1. Eisenhower consistently frames the issue of desegregation as one of obedience to law, rather than as a moral issue. Why do you think this is?
2. How does Eisenhower describe the white protesters in Little Rock, and how does this description lend support to his position?
3. What advantage is there for Eisenhower, in describing the situation in Little Rock as a local rather than a state problem?

Excerpted from Dwight D. Eisenhower's address to the United States, September 24, 1957.

My Fellow Citizens:

For a few minutes I want to speak to you about the serious situation that has arisen in Little Rock. For this talk I have come to the President's office in the White House. I could have spoken from Rhode Island, but I felt that, in speaking from the house of Lincoln, of Jackson and of Wilson, my words would more clearly convey both the sadness I feel in the action I was compelled today to take and the firmness with which I intend to pursue this course until the orders of the Federal Court at Little Rock can be executed without unlawful interference.

In that city, under the leadership of demagogic extremists, disorderly mobs have deliberately prevented the carrying out of proper orders from a Federal Court. Local authorities have not eliminated that violent opposition and, under the law, I yesterday issued a Proclamation calling upon the mob to disperse.

This morning the mob again gathered in front of the Central High School of Little Rock, obviously for the purpose of again preventing the carrying out of the Court's order relating to the admission of Negro children to the school.

Whenever normal agencies prove inadequate to the task and it becomes necessary for the Executive Branch of the Federal Government to use its powers and authority to uphold Federal Courts, the President's responsibility is inescapable.

In accordance with that responsibility, I have today issued an Executive Order directing the use of troops under Federal authority to aid in the execution of Federal law at Little Rock, Arkansas. This became necessary when my Proclamation of yesterday was not observed, and the obstruction of justice still continues.

It is important that the reasons for my action be understood by all citizens.

As you know, the Supreme Court of the United States has decided that separate public educational facilities for the races are inherently unequal and therefore compulsory school segregation laws are unconstitutional.

A Question of Law, Not Opinion

Our personal opinions about the decision have no bearing on the matter of enforcement; the responsibility and authority of the Supreme Court to interpret the Constitution are clear. Local Federal Courts were instructed by the Supreme Court to issue such orders and decrees as might be necessary to achieve admission to public schools without regard to race—and with all deliberate speed.

During the past several years, many communities in our Southern States have instituted public school plans for gradual progress in the enrollment and attendance of school children of all races in order to bring themselves into compliance with the law of the land.

They thus demonstrated to the world that we are a nation in which laws, not men, are supreme.

I regret to say that this truth—the cornerstone of our liberties—was not observed in this instance.

It was my hope that this localized situation would be brought under control by city and State authorities. If the use of local police powers had been sufficient, our traditional method of leaving the problem in those hands would have been pursued. But when large gatherings of obstructionists made it impossible for the decrees of the Court to be carried out, both the law and the national interest demanded that the President take action.

Here is the sequence of events in the development of the Little Rock school case.

In May of 1955, the Little Rock School Board approved a moderate plan for the gradual desegregation of the public schools in that city. It provided that a start toward integration would be made at the present term in the high school, and that the plan would be in full operation by 1963. This plan was challenged in the courts by some who believed that the period of time as proposed was too long.

The United States Court at Little Rock, which has supervisory responsibility under the law for the plan of desegregation in the public schools, dismissed the challenge, thus approving a gradual rather than an abrupt change from the

White students and adults against integration protest outside of Little Rock Central High School in Arkansas.

existing system. It found that the school board had acted in good faith in planning for a public school system free from racial discrimination.

Since that time, the court has on three separate occasions issued orders directing that the plan be carried out. All persons were instructed to refrain from interfering with the efforts of the school board to comply with the law.

Defying the Law

Proper and sensible observance of the law then demanded the respectful obedience which the nation has a right to expect from all the people. This, unfortunately, has not been the case at Little Rock. Certain misguided persons, many of them imported into Little Rock by agitators, have insisted upon defying the law and have sought to bring it into disrepute. The orders of the court have thus been frustrated.

The very basis of our individual rights and freedoms is the certainty that the President and the Executive Branch of Government will support and insure the carrying out of the decisions of the Federal Courts, even, when necessary with all the means at the President's command.

Unless the President did so, anarchy would result.

There would be no security for any except that which each one of us could provide for himself.

The interest of the nation in the proper fulfillment of the law's requirements cannot yield to opposition and demonstrations by some few persons.

Mob rule cannot be allowed to override the decisions of the courts.

Let me make it very clear that Federal troops are not being used to relieve local and state authorities of their primary duty to preserve the peace and order of the community. Nor are the troops there for the purpose of taking over the responsibility of the School Board and the other responsible local officials in running Central High School. In the present case the troops are there, pursuant to law, solely for the purpose of preventing interference with the orders of the Court.

The proper use of the powers of the Executive Branch to enforce the orders of a Federal Court is limited to extraordinary and compelling circumstances. Manifestly, such an extreme situation has been created in Little Rock. This challenge must be met with such measures as will preserve to the people as a whole their lawfully-protected rights in a climate permitting their free and fair exercise.

The Law-Abiding Majority

The overwhelming majority of our people in every section of the country are united in their respect for observance of the law—even in those cases where they may disagree with that law.

They deplore the call of extremists to violence.

The decision of the Supreme Court concerning school integration affects the South more seriously than it does other sections of the country. In that region I have many warm friends, some of them in the city of Little Rock. I have deemed it a great personal privilege to spend in our Southland tours of duty while in the military service and enjoyable recreational periods since that time.

So from intimate personal knowledge, I know that the overwhelming majority of the people in the South—including those of Arkansas and of Little Rock—are of good will, united in their efforts to preserve and respect the law even when they disagree with it.

They do not sympathize with mob rule. They, like the rest of the nation, have proved in two great wars their readiness to sacrifice for America.

A foundation of our American way of life is our national respect for law.

In the South, as elsewhere, citizens are keenly aware of the tremendous disservice that has been done to the people of Arkansas in the eyes of the nation, and that has been done to the nation in the eyes of the world.

At a time when we face a grave situation abroad because of the hatred that Communism bears toward a system of government based on human rights, it would be difficult to exaggerate the harm that is being done to the prestige and influence, and indeed to the safety, of our nation and the world.

Our enemies are gloating over this incident and using it everywhere to misrepresent our nation. We are portrayed as a violator of those standards of conduct which the peoples of the world united to proclaim in the Charter of the United Nations. There they affirmed "faith in fundamental human rights and in the dignity of the human person" and did so "without distinction as to race, sex, language or religion."

And so, with confidence, I call upon citizens of the State of Arkansas to assist in bringing to an immediate end all interference with the law and its processes. If resistance to the Federal Court orders ceases at once, the further presence of Federal troops will be unnecessary and the City of Little Rock will return to its normal habits of peace and order and a blot upon the fair name and high honor of our nation in the world will be removed.

Thus will be restored the image of America and of all its parts as one nation, indivisible, with liberty and justice for all.

The Federal Government Does Not Fight for Desegregation

Howard Zinn

In the late 1950s, and particularly the early 1960s under President John F. Kennedy, the federal government was seen by many as a strong advocate of civil rights and as a major force for segregation. This 1962 article, originally published in the *Nation*, by Howard Zinn, argues that the Kennedy administration was not, contrary to popular opinion, a dependable ally in the fight for civil rights. Zinn argues that the chief concern of the federal government seemed to be with preserving "law and order" rather than with serving justice. Zinn compares the federal response in Oxford, Mississippi, where President Kennedy stepped in with federal troops to ensure James Meredith, who was black, could enroll and attend class safely, to the federal response to events in Albany, Georgia. There, on two separate occasions, peaceful black protesters were rounded up by police and imprisoned, and the federal government did little in response. Furthermore, Zinn argues, various branches of the federal government, including the Federal Bureau of Investigation, seem to have been biased in favor of the white segregationists. Zinn believes that the federal government has been willing to intervene in the civil rights movements only when it was politically expedient, as when the well-known Martin Luther King Jr. was imprisoned, or when it could focus on procedural, rather than moral issues. At the time he wrote this piece, Zinn was chairman of the Department of History and Social Science at Spelman College.

Excerpted from "Kennedy, The Reluctant Emancipator," by Howard Zinn, *Nation*, December 1, 1962. Copyright © 1962 by the *Nation*. Reprinted with permission.

As you read, consider the following questions:
1. According to Zinn, what are the limits the Kennedy administration set for itself in dealing with desegregation?
2. Why does Zinn think the federal government was especially justified in intervening in Albany, Georgia?
3. Zinn criticizes the federal government for focusing on procedural rather than moral questions. Is there any reason for thinking, however, that governments should not involve themselves in moral questions?

The dispatch of federal troops to Oxford, Mississippi, tends to obscure the true cautiousness of John F. Kennedy in the movement for Negro rights. Oxford diverted attention from Albany, Georgia. In the former, the national government moved boldly and with overwhelming force. In the latter, which twice this past year has been the scene of Negro demonstrations, mass arrests and official violence, the federal government showed cautiousness to the point of timidity. The two situations, occurring in comparable Black Belt areas, point up the ambiguous, uncomfortable role of the Administration in civil rights. Oxford is fresh in the memory today and has been the object of an international uproar. Albany, now in the backwash of national attention, deserves to be brought forward for a good look.

I had the benefit of two such looks: last December, when that Black Belt city erupted with racial demonstrations for the first time in a long history going back to slavery days; and again last summer, when trouble burst out once more. Both times, the Southern Regional Council, which studies race matters throughout the South from its headquarters in Atlanta, had asked me to investigate and report. What I saw convinced me that the national government has an undeserved reputation, both among Southern opponents and Northern supporters, as a vigorous combatant for Negro rights.

To be fair, this much should be said at the outset in behalf of the Administration: fundamentally, it is behaving no differently from any of its precedessors. We have always lived in a white society, where even liberalism is tinged with whiteness. I am measuring the actions of the Kennedys not against past performances, but against the needs of our time. My object is not to denounce, but to clarify. It is important for American citizens to know exactly how far they can depend on the national government, and how much remains for them to do. In the field of racial equality, this government simply cannot be depended upon for vigorous initiatives. It will, however, respond to popular indignation and pressure. When I say that it often responds slowly and reluctantly, my intention is not to vilify John F. Kennedy, but to light a flame under the rest of us.

The Kennedy Administration has set limits, never publicized but nevertheless implicit in its actions, to its own power in the field of desegregation. It will act to keep law and order in cases of extreme and admitted defiance of federal authority, as in Oxford. But it will not act against violation of federal law in other cases—in Albany, Georgia, for instance—where the circumstances are less stark.

Law and Order

There is a rough analogy between Lincoln's insistence (in that famous letter to Horace Greeley) that he was more concerned with *union* than with slavery, and Kennedy's unspoken but obvious preoccupation with *law and order* above either desegregation or the right of free assembly. This explains why the Justice Department, while over a period of nine months 1,000 Negroes were being jailed in Albany for peaceful demonstrations against racial discrimination, gave tacit support to the chief of police for maintaining "law and order." Only after eight months of pressure and complaint did it enter the picture as "friend of the court" in a defensive suit. But it never took the initiative in behalf of Albany Negroes.

The analogy with Lincoln is only a rough one because even the "law and order" principle is applied by Kennedy rather narrowly, with shadowy situations interpreted against the Negro rather than for him. In the case of Ole Miss [the University of Mississippi] the law was unquestionably clear and the imminence of disorder equally clear. But in Albany, there was legal doubt. True, there was an Interstate Commerce Commission ruling and explicit court decisions calling for desegregation of the bus and train terminals. But did not the chief of police say on three successive occasions, when arresting young people who had used the "white" section of the terminal, that it was not a matter of race, but of keeping "order"? A forthright national government might have dismissed this argument as easily as it did Barnett's contention that race was not the basic reason for barring James Meredith from Ole Miss. But the Kennedy Administration chose not to challenge Albany's Chief Pritchett.

And when, last December, more than 700 Negro men, women and children were packed into jails in the Albany area for protesting segregation by marching through downtown streets and holding prayer meetings in front of City Hall, the government might have gone to court, on the basis of the First Amendment, to defend the right of free assembly. It might be contended, however, that with Negroes in jail, Albany had more "order." Also, constitutional lawyers disagree over the right of the government to take the initiative in enforcing the First Amendment. The Kennedy Administration has talked of the New Frontier, but perhaps this frontier does not extend into the South or into the field of constitutional law.

Hostile Police

Albany is a quiet commercial town in southwest Georgia surrounded by farm land that, in pre–Civil War days, was slave plantation country. Negroes, once a majority in the community, now make up 40 per cent of its population of 56,000. Interestingly enough, like many Southern cities just beginning the process of desegregation, Albany has been free of white mob violence of the kind that made headlines at Oxford, Little Rock and a few other places. When, last December, Negroes marched downtown in large but peaceful

An officer arrests Martin Luther King Jr. for leading an antisegregation march in Birmingham, Alabama.

groups to sing and pray in front of City Hall, whites stood by and watched with curiosity—resentful, perhaps, but quiet. It was the city and county officials who, by jailing the peaceful demonstrators, repeatedly violated the Fourteenth Amendment, which not only prohibits the application of local law on the basis of color, but also—according to constitutional doctrine accepted since the 1920s—bars deprivation by local officials of the rights of free speech, assembly and petition.

The fact that it was local police who violated constitutional doctrine is important because it is against local governments, rather than private persons, that the federal government has the clearest right to act in defense of the rights of citizens.

A shaky truce ended the December demonstrations, which had been provoked by arrests at the train terminal, but were rooted, of course, in the total segregation and white domination that make Albany, Georgia, such a hard place for Negroes to live in. By January, the truce began to fall apart. That month, an eighteen-year-old Negro girl named Ola Mae Quarterman sat in the front seat of an Albany bus, refused to move on the command of the driver, was arrested by a policeman and convicted in city court for using "obscene" language. The driver testified that she had told him: "I paid my damn twenty cents, and I can sit where I want." Subsequently Miss Quarterman told a federal court, to which her case had gone on appeal, that she had used the word "damn" in relation to her twenty cents, not in relation to the driver. (Anywhere but in the Deep South a judge might have thought it incredible that she should be forced to defend her words by making such a distinction.) The city's counsel insisted her race had nothing to do with her arrest, and in cross-examination asked if it were not true that the cause of her arrest was her "vulgar language." She replied softly, "That's what they said."

A Rash of Arrests

There followed several hundred arrests as the city police moved promptly against every Negro who, in any way and under any circumstances, challenged segregation patterns: two young men who sat in the Trailways terminal restaurant; four men picketing a store downtown; thirty youngsters asking service at a lunch counter; twenty-nine people praying in front of City Hall; thirty-two Negroes on the way to City Hall; 150 more on the way to City Hall; seven praying in front of City Hall; ten more, eighteen more, sixteen more, all praying in front of City Hall; fourteen praying at the Carnegie Library—all thrown into jail.

After a thousand arrests, Police Chief Laurie Pritchett emerged into national prominence as some sort of hero. He had kept the peace. Somehow, the standard for American democracy accepted by the Administration became the standard for the nation: the sole criterion was the prevention of violence. The fact that violence had at no time been imminent in the demonstrations was overlooked.

There is a statute in the U.S. Criminal Code, Section 242, going back to 1866, which makes it a crime for a local law-enforcement officer deliberately to subject "any inhabitant of any State . . . to the deprivation of any rights, privileges, or immunities secured or protected by the Constitution and laws of the United States. . . ." Under any reasonable interpretation, this law was broken in Albany at least thirty times from November 1, 1961, when police for the first time ignored the ICC [Interstate Commerce Commission] ruling desegregating the bus terminal, to the middle of August, 1962, when three youngsters trying to attend service at a white church were arrested. To select one instance with at least fifty witnesses: a county judge watched quietly from his bench as deputy sheriffs dragged and pushed out of his courtroom five young people—one Negro and four whites—who had taken seats in the "wrong" section (by race). One was a young woman whom a deputy dragged over a row of seats and pushed through a revolving door.

The U.S. Department of Justice maintains an FBI office in Albany. Affidavits have flowed into that FBI office in a steady stream, attesting to violations by local officials of the constitutional rights of Negroes. But nothing was done. As recently as last week, the Rev. Martin Luther King, Jr., publicly charged that the FBI agents in Albany have been favoring the segregationists. . . .

The Department of Justice, citing a 1943 case in which the conviction of a Georgia sheriff in the brutal killing of a Negro named Bobby Hall was overturned by a narrow Supreme Court interpretation of Section 242, takes the position that it should prosecute only in *extreme* cases of police brutality. This policy allows transgressors of Negro rights who stop short of premeditated murder to act with reasonable assurance that the federal government will not move. Last summer, at least three acts of brutality occurred in the Albany area, were duly reported to the FBI, and thus far have resulted in no federal action. I will describe these three in some detail as told to me by the principals.

Abuse Ignored
On July 23, 1962, about 5:30 P.M., Mrs. Slater King, wife of a Negro leader in the Albany Movement, drove from Al-

bany to the Camilla jail in neighboring Mitchell County, carrying food to a girl who had been arrested with a hundred other Negroes while on a march to City Hall. Mrs. King was in her sixth month of pregnancy, and had her three children along. "All you niggers get away from the fence," one of the deputies standing nearby called out as a group of visiting women approached the jailhouse. Mrs. King walked slowly towards her car. A deputy pointed her out, cursed her, threatened to arrest her if she didn't hurry. She turned and said, "If you want to arrest me, go ahead." She was then kicked, hit twice on the side of the head and was knocked unconscious.

Several days later, William Hansen, a twenty-year-old white field worker for the Student Non-Violent Coordinating Committee, and a veteran of jails in Mississippi and Maryland for participating in desegregation actions, was put in the Dougherty County jail in Albany after a prayer session in front of City Hall. A prison trustee, to whom the jailer had earlier suggested that Hansen needed to be "straightened out," beat the Cincinnati youth into senselessness as he sat on the floor reading. His jaw and several ribs were broken. Bleeding profusely from the mouth, he asked the jailer for medical aid, and was told this was not within the jailer's jurisdiction. Finally, a message shouted through the cell window brought about his transfer to the city jail, where he was hospitalized.

That same Saturday afternoon, C.B. King, thirty-six, the first and only Negro attorney in the city of Albany and the legal backbone of the Albany Movement, heard of Hansen's beating. He visited Sheriff Cull Campbell of Dougherty County to check on Hansen's condition. A Negro minister who was waiting to meet King in the Sheriff's office at the time later described what happened. Sheriff Campbell, seeing King in his office, said, "Nigger, haven't I told you to wait outside?" As King turned to reply, the Sheriff picked up a walking stick and hit him viciously on the head, breaking the cane. King staggered from the office, blood streaming from his head and crossed the street to

City Hall, where Chief Pritchett had him taken to a hospital. Pritchett, who had just arrested twenty-eight Negroes for praying and singing in front of City Hall, called the beating of King "very regrettable." *The New York Times* reporter, Claude Sitton, noted that "Chief Pritchett had more than 160 city, county and state law-enforcement officers standing by to prevent violence." Sheriff Campbell readily admitted the beating, when I questioned him a month after the incident: "Yeh, I knocked hell out of him, and I'll do it again. I let him know I'm a white man and he's a damn nigger."

All of the above three incidents were reported to the FBI, which dutifully recorded them. Thus far, the federal government has taken no action.

The few things that the national government *did* do in Albany give a clue to the boundaries it has drawn for itself in the field of civil rights. It went into a frantic day of telephone calls when Martin Luther King, Jr., was jailed in Albany; King, of course, is a politically important symbol. President Kennedy, in answer to questions on Albany at two different press conferences, made two statements. In one, he criticized Albany officials for refusing to negotiate with Negroes; in the other, he denounced the burning of Negro churches that had been used for voter-registration activities in the Albany area. The President's plea for negotiation, like his careful speech on the eve of Meredith's registration at Ole Miss, carefully skirted the moral issue of racial equality and stuck to procedural questions: the law, negotiation. The President has still not followed the advice of his own Civil Rights Commission to give "moral leadership" and to use "education and persuasion." His statement on church-burning covered two points on which the Administration is especially sensitive: its antipathy to nationally publicized violence and its careful defense of voting rights (but not other rights) guaranteed by the Constitution. The only federal suit initiated by the Justice Department in the Albany area was in defense of voter-registration activity.

There is a plausible legal argument to the effect that voting rights are protected by specific legislation (the Civil Rights Acts of 1957 and 1960), while the First Amendment rights of free speech, assembly, etc., and the Fourteenth Amendment right to color-blind treatment by local officials, are not. However, a national administration less timorous than the present one could find solid legal sanction for the widespread use of injunctions to protect free assembly and to attack legal segregation. In the Debs case of 1895, the Supreme Court supported the issuance of injunctions without specific statutory basis, saying: "Every government has a right to apply to its own courts in matters which the Constitution has entrusted to the care of the national government." This ruling has never been overturned.

A truly bold national administration might do the following: (1) prosecute vigorously, under Sec. 242, violations of Negro rights by local officers; (2) create a corps of special agents—not encumbered, as is the FBI, by intimate relations with local police officers—to prevent, as well as to investigate, violations of constitutional rights; (3) use the power of injunction freely, both to prevent policemen from curtailing the right of assembly and petition and to break down legal enforcement of segregation; (4) tell the South and the nation frankly that racial discrimination is morally wrong as well as illegal, and that the nation intends to wipe it out.

At this moment, because of the limitations that the Administration has imposed upon itself, there is a vast no-man's-land for American Negroes into which they are invited by the Constitution, but where federal authority will not protect them. It was into this no-man's-land that the Negro population of Albany ventured, and found itself deserted. The future may bring one or two more Oxfords, but there are a hundred potential Albanys. Throughout the Deep South, Negroes are on the move towards dangerous territory. And so far, though these men, women and children live in a nation whose power encircles the globe and reaches into space, they are very much on their own.

Segregation Is Morally Wrong and Must End

John F. Kennedy

Although the Supreme Court's 1954 decision in *Brown v. Board of Education* struck down state-enforced segregation in public schools, schools in Alabama remained totally segregated until 1963, when George C. Wallace became governor on a pledge to "stand in the schoolhouse door" to bar black students from entering white schools. In early June 1963, Wallace went to the University of Alabama with the Alabama National Guard in order to block two black students, Vivian Malone and James Hood, from enrolling. When Wallace stopped the students and officials from the Justice Department at the entrance to the registration building, President John F. Kennedy intervened, taking the Guard under his command and ordering them to ensure the students were enrolled. Later that day, in an address broadcast nationwide on television and radio, Kennedy called segregation a moral issue confronting the entire country. In this speech, reprinted below, Kennedy speaks in unequivocal terms about the need for federal action to end segregation, and he asks for support from the citizenry and from Congress for new federal laws barring segregation in public places.

As you read, consider the following questions:
1. Why does Kennedy frame the issue of segregation as a national problem?
2. What reasons does Kennedy give for thinking segregation is a moral issue rather than merely a legal issue?
3. How does Kennedy contrast American efforts abroad with the situation at home?

Excerpted from John F. Kennedy's address to the American people, June 11, 1963.

This afternoon, following a series of threats and defiant statements, the presence of Alabama National Guardsmen was required on the University of Alabama to carry out the final and unequivocal order of the United States District Court of the Northern District of Alabama. That order called for the admission of two clearly qualified young Alabama residents who happened to have been born Negro.

That they were admitted peacefully on the campus is due in good measure to the conduct of the students of the University of Alabama, who met their responsibilities in a constructive way.

I hope that every American, regardless of where he lives, will stop and examine his conscience about this and other related incidents. This Nation was founded by men of many nations and backgrounds. It was founded on the principle that all men are created equal, and that the rights of every man are diminished when the rights of one man are threatened.

Today we are committed to a worldwide struggle to promote and protect the rights of all who wish to be free. And when Americans are sent to Viet-Nam or West Berlin, we do not ask for whites only. It ought to be possible, therefore, for American students of any color to attend any public institution they select without having to be backed up by troops.

It ought to be possible for American consumers of any color to receive equal service in places of public accommodation, such as hotels and restaurants and theaters and retail stores, without being forced to resort to demonstrations in the street, and it ought to be possible for American citizens of any color to register to vote in a free election without interference or fear of reprisal.

It ought to be possible, in short, for every American to enjoy the privileges of being American without regard to his race or his color. In short, every American ought to have the right to be treated as he would wish to be treated, as one would wish his children to be treated. But this is not the case.

The Negro baby born in America today, regardless of the section of the Nation in which he is born, has about one-half as much chance of completing a high school as a white baby born in the same place on the same day, one-third as much chance of completing college, one-third as much chance of becoming a professional man, twice as much chance of becoming unemployed, about one-seventh as much chance of earning $10,000 a year, a life expectancy which is 7 years shorter, and the prospects of earning only half as much.

This is not a sectional issue. Difficulties over segregation and discrimination exist in every city, in every State of the Union, producing in many cities a rising tide of discontent that threatens the public safety. Nor is this a partisan issue. In a time of domestic crisis men of good will and generosity should be able to unite regardless of party or politics. This is not even a legal or legislative issue alone. It is better to settle these matters in the courts than on the streets, and new laws are needed at every level, but law alone cannot make men see right.

A Moral Issue

We are confronted primarily with a moral issue. It is as old as the scriptures and is as clear as the American Constitution.

The heart of the question is whether all Americans are to be afforded equal rights and equal opportunities, whether we are going to treat our fellow Americans as we want to be treated. If an American, because his skin is dark, cannot eat lunch in a restaurant open to the public, if he cannot send his children to the best public school available, if he cannot vote for the public officials who will represent him, if, in short, he cannot enjoy the full and free life which all of us want, then who among us would be content to have the color of his skin changed and stand in his place? Who among us would then be content with the counsels of patience and delay?

One hundred years of delay have passed since President Lincoln freed the slaves, yet their heirs, their grandsons, are not fully free. They are not yet freed from the bonds of injustice. They are not yet freed from social and economic oppression. And this Nation, for all its hopes and all its boasts, will not be fully free until all its citizens are free.

We preach freedom around the world, and we mean it, and we cherish our freedom here at home, but are we to say to the world, and much more importantly, to each other that this is the land of the free except for the Negroes; that we have no second-class citizens except Negroes; that we have no class or caste system, no ghettoes, no master race except with respect to Negroes?

Now the time has come for this Nation to fulfill its promise. The events in Birmingham and elsewhere have so increased the cries for equality that no city or State or legislative body can prudently choose to ignore them.

The fires of frustration and discord are burning in every city, North and South, where legal remedies are not at hand. Redress is sought in the streets, in demonstrations, parades, and protests which create tensions and threaten violence and threaten lives.

We face, therefore, a moral crisis as a country and as a people. It cannot be met by repressive police action. It cannot be left to increased demonstrations in the streets. It cannot be quieted by token moves or talk. It is time to act in the Congress, in your State and local legislative body and, above all, in all of our daily lives.

It is not enough to pin the blame of others, to say this is a problem of one section of the country or another, or deplore the fact that we face. A great change is at hand, and our task, our obligation, is to make that revolution, that change, peaceful and constructive for all.

Those who do nothing are inviting shame as well as violence. Those who act boldly are recognizing right as well as reality.

A Time for Action

Next week I shall ask the Congress of the United States to act, to make a commitment it has not fully made in this century to the proposition that race has no place in American life or law. The Federal judiciary has upheld that proposition in the conduct of its affairs, including the employment of Federal personnel, the use of Federal facilities, and the sale of federally financed housing.

But there are other necessary measures which only the Congress can provide, and they will be provided at this session. The old code of equity law under which we live commands for every wrong a remedy, but in too many communities, in too many parts of the country, wrongs are inflicted on Negro citizens and there are no remedies at law. Unless the Congress acts, their only remedy is in the street.

I am, therefore, asking the Congress to enact legislation giving all Americans the right to be served in facilities which are open to the public—hotels, restaurants, theaters, retail stores, and similar establishments.

This seems to me to be an elementary right. Its denial is an arbitrary indignity that no American in 1963 should have to endure, but many do.

I have recently met with scores of business leaders urging them to take voluntary action to end this discrimination and I have been encouraged by their response, and in the last 2 weeks over 75 cities have seen progress made in desegregating these kinds of facilities. But many are unwilling to act alone, and for this reason, nationwide legislation is needed if we are to move this problem from the streets to the courts.

I am also asking the Congress to authorize the Federal Government to participate more fully in lawsuits designed to end segregation in public education. We have succeeded in persuading many districts to desegregate voluntarily. Dozens have admitted Negroes without violence. Today a Negro is attending a State-supported institution in every one of our 50 States, but the pace is very slow.

Too many Negro children entering segregated grade schools at the time of the Supreme Court's decision 9 years ago will enter segregated high schools this fall, having suffered a loss which can never be restored. The lack of an adequate education denies the Negro a chance to get a decent job.

The orderly implementation of the Supreme Court decision, therefore, cannot be left solely to those who may not have the economic resources to carry the legal action or who may be subject to harassment.

Other features will also be requested, including greater protection for the right to vote. But legislation, I repeat, cannot solve this problem alone. It must be solved in the homes of every American in every community across our country.

A Problem for All

In this respect I want to pay tribute to those citizens North and South who have been working in their communities to make life better for all. They are acting not out of a sense of legal duty but out of a sense of human decency.

Like our soldiers and sailors in all parts of the world they are meeting freedom's challenge on the firing line, and I salute them for their honor and their courage.

My fellow Americans, this is a problem which faces us all—in every city of the North as well as the South. Today there are Negroes unemployed, two or three times as many compared to whites, inadequate in education, moving into the large cities, unable to find work, young people particularly out of work without hope, denied equal rights, denied the opportunity to eat at a restaurant or lunch counter or go to a movie theater, denied the right to a decent education, denied almost today the right to attend a State university even though qualified. It seems to me that these are matters which concern us all, not merely Presidents or Congressmen or Governors, but every citizen of the United States.

This is one country. It has become one country because all of us and all the people who came here had an equal chance to develop their talents.

We cannot say to 10 percent of the population that you can't have that right; that your children cannot have the chance to develop whatever talents they have; that the only way that they are going to get their rights is to go into the streets and demonstrate. I think we owe them and we owe ourselves a better country than that.

Therefore, I am asking for your help in making it easier for us to move ahead and to provide the kind of equality of treatment which we would want ourselves; to give a chance for every child to be educated to the limit of his talents.

As I have said before, not every child has an equal talent or an equal ability or an equal motivation, but they should have an equal right to develop their talent and their ability and their motivation, to make something of themselves.

We have a right to expect that the Negro community will be responsible, will uphold the law, but they have a right to expect that the law will be fair, that the Constitution will be color blind, as Justice Harlan said at the turn of the century.

This is what we are talking about and this is a matter which concerns this country and what it stands for, and in meeting it I ask the support of all our citizens.

Thank you very much.

3

THE PLACE
OF PROTEST

CHAPTER PREFACE

Protests played a key role in the civil rights movement and in the desegregation of schools, businesses, and transportation. Protests took two forms. In one, concerned citizens protested in the streets, exercising their constitutional rights of free speech and free assembly to gather and express their displeasure with prevailing law or custom. Such protests occurred countless times at the state houses and in the public squares of the South. Perhaps the most famous of these protests was the 1963 March on Washington, during which Martin Luther King Jr. delivered his "I Have a Dream" speech while standing in the shadow of the Lincoln Memorial. Another form of protest, known as direct action or nonviolent resistance, was also used by those in favor of desegregation. In this form of protest, activists peacefully violated laws that they considered unjust and allowed themselves to be arrested—and, on many occasions, quite openly brutalized by the police. The goal of such protests was to highlight the injustice of discriminatory laws and appeal to the conscience of observers, the ordinary men and women of America who watched, with varying degrees of shock or horror, the events unfolding on their television screens. This second form of protest, because it emphasized the violation of law and was likely to end in violence, was controversial.

Those who practiced direct action and nonviolent resistance drew their inspiration from Mohandas Gandhi, whose peaceful protests in India against British rule had been instrumental in gaining national independence. Just as the success of Gandhi hinged on the British reluctance to attack unarmed and peaceful citizens, the American protesters hoped that, by refusing to defend themselves, they would ultimately prevail. As they saw it, breaking the law peacefully was a noble and justified act. An unjust law, such as one that was discriminatory and racist, was not a law that deserved to be obeyed, they reasoned. Furthermore, although such protests often ended in violence, in almost all cases the violence was perpetrated by angry white citizens or enraged white police officers. According to the protesters, they were not responsible for the violence that ensued. Indeed, it was argued that nonviolent protests, when they provoked violence by whites, only brought the latent violence of racism to the surface. The protesters believed that they had willingly made themselves the victims of violence as a means of asserting the moral high ground, so they could not be held responsible for initiating protests that ended up harming other parties. In this chapter, Martin Luther King Jr., Diane Nash, and Patricia Stephens offer this view of the protests. A different view is offered by Jan Howard, who argues that violence was an important part of such protests, whatever may have been said to the contrary. She believes that such protests worked only when violence ensued, and argues that, on occasion, those in the nonviolence movement actively sought violence.

There are two other important features of nonviolent resistance. The first is that those who practiced it were often, although by no means exclusively, religious, and especially Christian. Furthermore, they often saw their involvement in such protests in spiritual terms, and spoke of countering violence with "soul force." The idea was that Christian love, exemplified by the belief that, when struck, one is to offer one's other cheek to the aggressor, would prevail over racist hatred. The protests also often took on a religious character because the church played a major role in black life in the South and was often the focal point of organized black political activity. And black community leaders, such as the Reverend Martin Luther King Jr., were often religious leaders.

The second important feature of nonviolent resistance is that it was a new strategy and a sharp departure from the legal strategies emphasized by the National Association for the Advancement of Colored People and other civil rights groups. Students and other young people played an instrumental role in nonviolent protests, not merely as participants but as organizers, and some saw in the protests youthful frustration with the gradualism of established civil rights groups. Furthermore, it was argued, the protests were a popular movement, and thus reflected a certain maturity among the black population, which no longer saw itself as needing to speak and act through leaders. This view is offered by Louis E. Lomax.

Although the whites in the South who responded to the protests with violence commanded most of the national attention, far larger was the group of white citizens who did not play an overtly active part in either promoting or resisting desegregation. Although it would be a mistake to characterize them as detached observers, for they had varying degrees of enthusiasm for or concern about segregation and were deeply involved in the system of racial separation, they often saw themselves as part of, rather than responsible for, a complex structure that oppressed blacks. In the following chapter, Robert Coles discusses the perspective of the "ordinary white."

The Way to Justice Is Nonviolent Resistance

Martin Luther King Jr.

In this selection, Martin Luther King Jr. explains and defends the philosophy of nonviolent resistance, which was used with great success by opponents of segregation. People who are oppressed, King argues, have a moral obligation to resist oppression, yet both justice and prudence demands that they shun violence. When oppressed people turn to violence, King reasons, they wrongly rely on hatred rather than love, and engender bitterness, leading to a spiral of retaliatory violence. In contrast, nonviolent resistance, which King adopts from the Indian pacifist Mohandas Gandhi, is designed to highlight, in a just way, the barbarity of the oppressor. This selection is drawn from King's 1958 book *Stride Toward Freedom*, which recounts the successful boycott of the Montgomery bus system. Nonviolent resistance was a key tactic in the South in the late 1950s and early 1960s, and King is generally regarded as the principal figure in that movement. He was awarded the Nobel Peace Prize in 1963 and assassinated in 1968, in Memphis, Tennessee, where he was supporting striking garbage workers.

As you read, consider the following questions:
1. Why does King believe that the struggle is not between white and black Americans, but between justice and injustice?
2. Does the approach King advocates work only if the oppressor resorts to violence?

Excerpted from *Stride Toward Freedom: The Montgomery Story*, by Martin Luther King Jr. (New York: Harper and Brothers Publishers, 1958). Copyright © 1958 by Martin Luther King Jr. Reprinted by permission of the publisher.

3. For King, would successful desegregation count as victory, or is something else required?

The Negro himself has a decisive role to play if integration is to become a reality. Indeed, if first-class citizenship is to become a reality for the Negro he must assume the primary responsibility for making it so. Integration is not some lavish dish that the federal government or the white liberal will pass out on a silver platter while the Negro merely furnishes the appetite. One of the most damaging effects of past segregation on the personality of the Negro may well be that he has been victimized with the delusion that others should be more concerned than himself about his citizenship rights.

In this period of social change, the Negro must come to see that there is much he himself can do about his plight. He may be uneducated or poverty-stricken, but these handicaps must not prevent him from seeing that he has within his being the power to alter his fate. The Negro can take direct action against injustice without waiting for the government to act or a majority to agree with him or a court to rule in his favor.

Oppressed people deal with their oppression in three characteristic ways. One way is acquiescence: the oppressed resign themselves to their doom. They tacitly adjust themselves to oppression, and thereby become conditioned to it. In every movement toward freedom some of the oppressed prefer to remain oppressed. Almost 2800 years ago Moses set out to lead the children of Israel from the slavery of Egypt to the freedom of the promised land. He soon discovered that slaves do not always welcome their deliverers. They become accustomed to being slaves. They would rather bear those ills they have, as Shakespeare pointed out, than flee to others that they know not of. They prefer the "fleshpots of Egypt" to the ordeals of emancipation.

There is such a thing as the freedom of exhaustion. Some people are so worn down by the yoke of oppression that they give up. A few years ago in the slum areas of Atlanta, a Negro guitarist used to sing almost daily: "Ben down so long that down don't bother me." This is the type of negative freedom and resignation that often engulfs the life of the oppressed.

Justice Demands Resistance

But this is not the way out. To accept passively an unjust system is to coöperate with that system; thereby the oppressed become as evil as the oppressor. Noncoöperation with evil is as much a moral obligation as is coöperation with good. The oppressed must never allow the conscience of the oppressor to slumber. Religion reminds every man that he is his brother's keeper. To accept injustice or segregation passively is to say to the oppressor that his actions are morally right. It is a way of allowing his conscience to fall asleep. At this moment the oppressed fails to be his brother's keeper. So acquiescence—while often the easier way—is not the moral way. It is the way of the coward. The Negro cannot win the respect of his oppressor by acquiescing; he merely increases the oppressor's arrogance and contempt. Acquiescence is interpreted as proof of the Negro's inferiority. The Negro cannot win the respect of the white people of the South or the peoples of the world if he is willing to sell the future of his children for his personal and immediate comfort and safety.

A second way that oppressed people sometimes deal with oppression is to resort to physical violence and corroding hatred. Violence often brings about momentary results. Nations have frequently won their independence in battle. But in spite of temporary victories, violence never brings permanent peace. It solves no social problem; it merely creates new and more complicated ones.

Violence as a way of achieving racial justice is both impractical and immoral. It is impractical because it is a descending spiral ending in destruction for all. The old law of an eye for an eye leaves everybody blind. It is immoral because it seeks to humiliate the opponent rather than win his understanding; it seeks to annihilate rather than to convert. Violence is immoral because it thrives on hatred rather than love. It destroys community and makes broth-

Martin Luther King Jr.

erhood impossible. It leaves society in monologue rather than dialogue. Violence ends by defeating itself. It creates bitterness in the survivors and brutality in the destroyers. A voice echoes through time saying to every potential Peter, "Put up your sword." History is cluttered with the wreckage of nations that failed to follow this command.

If the American Negro and other victims of oppression succumb to the temptation of using violence in the struggle for freedom, future generations will be the recipients of a desolate night of bitterness, and our chief legacy to them will be an endless reign of meaningless chaos. Violence is not the way.

The Only Path to Victory

The third way open to oppressed people in their quest for freedom is the way of nonviolent resistance. Like the synthesis in Hegelian philosophy, the principle of nonviolent resistance seeks to reconcile the truths of two opposites—acquiescence and violence—while avoiding the extremes and immoralities of both. The nonviolent resister agrees with the person who acquiesces that one should not be physically aggressive toward his opponent; but he balances the equation by agreeing with the person of violence that evil must be resisted. He avoids the nonresistance of the former and the violent resistance of the latter. With nonviolent resistance, no individual or group need submit to any wrong, nor need anyone resort to violence in order to right a wrong.

It seems to me that this is the method that must guide the actions of the Negro in the present crisis in race relations. Through nonviolent resistance the Negro will be able to rise to the noble height of opposing the unjust system while loving the perpetrators of the system. The Negro must work passionately and unrelentingly for full stature as a citizen, but he must not use inferior methods to gain it. He must never come to terms with falsehood, malice, hate, or destruction.

Nonviolent resistance makes it possible for the Negro to remain in the South and struggle for his rights. The Negro's problem will not be solved by running away. He cannot listen to the glib suggestion of those who would urge him to migrate en masse to other sections of the country. By grasping his great opportunity in the South he can make a lasting contribution to the moral strength of the nation and set a sublime example of courage for generations yet unborn.

By nonviolent resistance, the Negro can also enlist all men of good will in his struggle for equality. The problem is not a purely racial one, with Negroes set against whites. In the end, it is not a struggle between people at all, but a tension between justice and injustice. Nonviolent resistance is not aimed against oppressors but against oppression. Under its banner consciences, not racial groups, are enlisted.

How Nonviolence Works

If the Negro is to achieve the goal of integration, he must organize himself into a militant and nonviolent mass movement. All three elements are indispensable. The movement for equality and justice can only be a success if it has both a mass and militant character; the barriers to be overcome require both. Nonviolence is an imperative in order to bring about ultimate community.

A mass movement of a militant quality that is not at the same time committed to nonviolence tends to generate conflict, which in turn breeds anarchy. The support of the participants and the sympathy of the uncommitted are both inhibited by the threat that bloodshed will engulf the community. This reaction in turn encourages the opposition to threaten and resort to force. When, however, the mass movement repudiates violence while moving resolutely toward its goal, its opponents are revealed as the instigators and practitioners of violence if it occurs. Then public support is magnetically attracted to the advocates of nonviolence, while those who employ violence are literally disarmed by overwhelming sentiment against their stand.

Only through a nonviolent approach can the fears of the white community be mitigated. A guilt-ridden white minority lives in fear that if the Negro should ever attain power, he would act without restraint or pity to revenge the injustices and brutality of the years. It is something like a parent who continually mistreats a son. One day that parent raises his hand to strike the son, only to discover that the son is now as tall as he is. The parent is suddenly afraid—fearful that the son will use his new physical power to repay his parent for all the blows of the past.

No Reason for Fear

The Negro, once a helpless child, has now grown up politically, culturally, and economically. Many white men fear retaliation. The job of the Negro is to show them that they have nothing to fear, that the Negro understands and forgives and is ready to forget the past. He must convince the white man that all he seeks is justice, *for both himself and the white man.* A mass movement exercising nonviolence is an object lesson in power under discipline, a demonstration to the white community that if such a movement attained a degree of strength, it would use its power creatively and not vengefully.

Nonviolence can touch men where the law cannot reach them. When the law regulates behavior it plays an indirect part in molding public sentiment. The enforcement of the law is itself a form of peaceful persuasion. But the law needs help. The courts can order desegregation of the public schools. But what can be done to mitigate the fears, to disperse the hatred, violence, and irrationality gathered around school integration, to take the initiative out of the hands of racial demagogues, to release respect for the law? In the end, for laws to be obeyed, men must believe they are right.

Here nonviolence comes in as the ultimate form of persuasion. It is the method which seeks to implement the just law by appealing to the conscience of the great decent majority who through blindness, fear, pride, or irrationality have allowed their consciences to sleep.

The nonviolent resisters can summarize their message in the following simple terms: We will take direct action against injustice without waiting for other agencies to act. We will not obey unjust laws or submit to unjust practices. We will do this peacefully, openly, cheerfully because our aim is to persuade. We adopt the means of nonviolence because our end is a community at peace with itself. We will try to persuade with our words, but if our words fail, we will try to persuade with our acts. We will always be willing to talk and seek fair compromise, but we are ready to suffer when necessary and even risk our lives to become witnesses to the truth as we see it.

A Willingness to Suffer

The way of nonviolence means a willingness to suffer and sacrifice. It may mean going to jail. If such is the case the resister must be willing to fill the jail houses of the South. It may even mean physical death. But if physical death is the price that a man must pay to free his children and his white brethren from a permanent death of the spirit, then nothing could be more redemptive.

What is the Negro's best defense against acts of violence inflicted upon him? As Dr. Kenneth Clark has said so eloquently, "His only defense is to meet every act of barbarity, illegality, cruelty and injustice toward an individual Negro with the fact that 100 more Negroes will present themselves in his place as potential victims." Every time one Negro school teacher is fired for believing in integration, a thousand others should be ready to take the same stand. If the oppressors bomb the home of one Negro for his protest, they must be made to realize that to press back the rising tide of the Negro's courage they will have to bomb hundreds more, and even then they will fail.

Faced with this dynamic unity, this amazing self-respect, this willingness to suffer, and this refusal to hit back, the oppressor will find, as oppressors have always found, that he is glutted with his own barbarity. Forced to stand before the world and his God splattered with the blood of his brother, he will call an end to his self-defeating massacre.

American Negroes must come to the point where they can say to their white brothers, paraphrasing the words of Gandhi: "We will match your capacity to inflict suffering with our capacity to endure suffering. We will meet your physical force with soul force. We will not hate you, but we cannot in all good conscience obey your unjust laws. Do to us what you will and we will still love you. Bomb our homes and threaten our children; send your hooded perpetrators of violence into our communities and drag us out on some wayside road, beating us and leaving us half dead, and we will still love you. But we will soon wear you down by our capacity to suffer. And in winning our freedom we will so appeal to your heart and conscience that we will win you in the process."

The Nonviolent Movement

Diane Nash

Diane Nash was raised in Chicago but became involved in the desegregation movement in 1961, while she was a student at Fisk University. In the following article she discusses her experiences in "Dixie," as the southern states were known. Nash calls the nonviolent movement "applied religion," reflecting the fact that a great many of those involved in the fight against segregation were deeply religious. According to Nash, the problem plaguing the South was ultimately the same as that which plagued many places around the world, and was an inability to see the "God within" each human being. For Nash, the goal of the protests was not merely to bring about desegregation, but was instead to create what was known as a "beloved community," in which the inherent dignity of all human beings is respected. Nash also discusses the Freedom Rides, in which whites and blacks rode buses together from Washington, D.C., into the Deep South, in an effort to integrate rest stops and terminals along the way. Nash's story is a stirring account of the danger the riders faced, and of the courage which, according to Nash, the sense of community and unity engendered.

As you read, consider the following questions:
1. Why does Nash think the same problem exists in Berlin, in Cuba, and in Jackson, Mississippi?
2. Why does Nash think that being involved in the desegregation movement helps instill courage in the hearts of black people in the South?
3. How does Nash respond to the accusation that nonviolent protesters are troublemakers who persist in their efforts even though their point has been made?

Excerpted from "Inside the Sit-Ins and Freedom Rides: Testimony of a Southern Student," by Diane Nash in *The New Negro*, edited by Mathew Ahmann (Notre Dame, IN: Fides Publishers, 1961). Copyright © 1961 by Fides Publishers. Reprinted with permission.

I see no alternative but that this text must be a personal interpretation of my own experience within the region known as "Dixie."

My participation in the movement began in February, 1960, with the lunch counter "sit-ins." I was then a student at Fisk University, but several months ago I interrupted my schoolwork for a year in order to work full time with the movement. My occupation at present is coordinating secretary for the Nashville Nonviolent Movement.

I should not wish to infer that I speak for the southern movement, for I think that there is no single person who can do that. Although many of the following statements can be generalized for the entire movement in the South, I shall refer largely to Nashville, Tennessee, for that is where I have worked.

I submit, then, that the nonviolent movement in that city:
1. is based upon and motivated by love;
2. attempts to serve God and mankind;
3. strives toward what we call the beloved community.

This is religion. This is applied religion. I think it has worked for me and I think it has worked for you and I think it is the work of our Church.

One fact occurs to me. This is that the problems of the world lie within men and women; yes, within you, me, and the people with whom we come in contact daily. Further, the problems lie not so much in our action as in our inaction. We have upon ourselves as individuals in a democracy the political, economic, sociological, and spiritual responsibilities of our country. I'm wondering now if we in the United States are really remembering that this must be a government "of the people" and "by the people" as well as "for the people." Are we really appreciating the fact that if you and I do not meet these responsibilities then our government *cannot* survive as a democracy?

The problems in Berlin, Cuba, or South Africa are, I think, identical with the problem in Jackson, Mississippi, or Nashville, Tennessee. I believe that when men come to believe in their own dignity and in the worth of their own freedom, and when they can acknowledge the God and the dignity that is within every man, then Berlin and Jackson will not be problems. After I had been arrested from a picket line about three weeks ago, I jotted down the following note, with this meeting in mind:

> If the policeman had acknowledged the God within each of the students with whom I was arrested last night, would he have put us in jail? Or would he have gone into the store we were picketing and tried to persuade the manager to hire Negroes and to treat all people fairly? If one acknowledges the God within men, would anyone ask for a "cooling off period," or plead for gradualism, or would they realize that white and Negro Americans are committing sin every day that they hate each other and every day that they allow an evil system to exist without doing all they can to rectify it as soon as they can?

Segregation reaches into every aspect of life to oppress the Negro and to rob him of his dignity in the South. The very fact that he is forced to be separated obviously implies his inferiority. Therefore the phrase "separate but equal" denies itself. The things non-black Americans take for granted, such as a movie and dinner date for college students, or a coffee-break downtown, are usually denied the black American in the South. Sometimes he may obtain these services if he wishes to compromise his dignity. He might, for example, attend a downtown movie if he would enter through the alley entrance and climb to the balcony to be seated.

But these are not the most important things. The purpose of the movement and of the sit-ins and the Freedom Rides and any other such actions, as I see it, is to bring about a climate in which all men are respected as men, in which there is appreciation of the dignity of man and in which each individual is free to grow and produce to his fullest capacity.

We of the movement often refer to this goal as the concept of the redeemed or the "beloved" community. . . .

A Trip Through the South

I am eager to talk with you about the Freedom Rides because I think that they denote a new and important level of effort. And I feel that more such projects will be necessary for the ultimate success of the southern movement, especially in states of the deep South, such as Alabama and Mississippi. As you know, the idea of a Freedom Ride was conceived and the project was begun by the Congress of Racial Equality. The first trip originated in Washington, D.C., in May of this year (1961). From Washington, the group traveled through most of the southern states and was repeatedly beaten and jailed as the bus made its way across Dixie. As you remember, at Anniston and Birmingham, Alabama, the bus met with mob violence; the CORE members were beaten and the bus was burned. Most of the riders were hospitalized for a short time. Mr. James Peck, who was one of the whites along with the group, had fifty stitches taken in his head as a result of the repeated beatings that he had to take. Attempting to get a bus to their destination, which was Montgomery, the riders were told that no driver would take them further. In a state of exhaustion then, after traveling hundreds of miles under tremendous tension, repeated jailings and beatings, they took a plane to New Orleans, which was the last stop of the planned itinerary.

In Nashville, the students had been closely following the Freedom Bus as it moved from town to town, for the people on the bus somehow were ourselves. Their dream of freedom in travel was our dream also. Their aspirations were our own aspirations. There is a tremendous bond between people who really stand up or ride for what they feel is just and right. You see, the CORE members were riding and being beaten for our freedom, too. Therefore, it was quite simple. Mob violence must not stop men's striving toward right. Freedom Rides and other such actions must not be stopped until our nation is really free.

In Nashville then, we were faced with a grave situation. We called a meeting of the students and adults within the movement. Talking by phone with persons who had been at the scene of the tragedies in Birmingham and Anniston, we were told, "Don't come. It's a bloodbath. Be assured, someone will be killed if you do come." Upon hearing this, the Nashville group set about preparing themselves for the fact that someone of them would be killed when they took the trip.

Facing Death

You see, these people faced the probability of their own deaths before they ever left Nashville. Several made out wills. A few more gave me sealed letters to be mailed if they were killed. Some told me frankly that they were afraid, but they knew that this was something that they must do because freedom was worth it. I, incidentally, feel very blessed and very grateful for knowing such people and for being able to call most of them my friends.

The purpose of any nonviolent demonstration is to focus the attention of people on how evil segregation really is and then to change their hearts. Some people have been confused about the objectives of the Freedom Rides, and I've heard it said that "the point has been made," so there is no use in going on. The objective of the Freedom Ride from Birmingham was not just to point out that people cannot ride freely but to make it possible for all persons to ride and use terminal facilities without being discriminated against. Until that objective has been attained there *is* reason for going on.

So the drama continued. The bus left Nashville about 6:00 A.M. en route to Birmingham, Alabama. My own role was to stay at the telephone, to keep contact with Birmingham, to hear from the riders as often as they could call, to make arrangements ahead in Montgomery, to keep the Justice Department advised—in short, to coordinate.

The students were held on the bus for some time when they reached Birmingham, and subsequently were taken into "protective custody." The next morning at 4:25, I re-

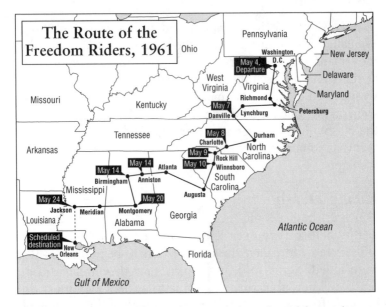

The Route of the Freedom Riders, 1961

Ohio
Pennsylvania
Washington, D.C.
May 4, Departure
New Jersey
Delaware
Maryland
West Virginia
Virginia
Richmond
Petersburg
Missouri
Kentucky
May 7
Danville
Lynchburg
Tennessee
May 8
Charlotte
Durham
North Carolina
Arkansas
May 9
Rock Hill
May 14
Atlanta
May 10
Winnsboro
South Carolina
May 14
Birmingham
Anniston
Augusta
Mississippi
May 20
May 24
Jackson
Meridian
Montgomery
Georgia
Louisiana
Alabama
Scheduled destination
New Orleans
Florida
Atlantic Ocean
Gulf of Mexico

ceived a call from them. They said that they'd been driven by the police to the Alabama-Tennessee border and had been put out of the car there on the highway and told to cross the border. At the moment they were on the open highway and felt unsafe. They did not know where shelter was, but would call again as soon as possible. They had been fasting since they had been in jail the day before.

We immediately sent an automobile to get them, and the next time we heard from them, they advised us that they were returning to Birmingham and were determined to board a bus for Montgomery. The police chief wasn't going to get off that easily.

The next night was an all-night vigil for them at the bus station. They were told, again, that no driver would drive the bus. Finally, next morning they were able to get a driver and the bus moved on to Montgomery, Alabama. We all read about that morning, I think, in Montgomery, Alabama. I wish I could have shared with you the moments in our office when that violence was taking place. It seemed that when the bus arrived and the mob attacked the students, they were immediately dispersed. People put a few of them in their cars and took them home. Within a very short time the group was scattered throughout the city.

A Tense Wait

We listed all the names of the persons who had left Nashville and began trying to account for them. We would ask the students as they called in, "When did you last see _____?" The reports we got that morning were: John Lewis was bleeding profusely from the head; another student seemed unconscious; Jim Swirg had been cornered by about sixteen or seventeen men and was being beaten. They had lead pipes, knives, and guns. In a relatively short time, however, we were able to account for all of the students. Miraculously, no one was dead.

Shortly afterwards, in the job of coordinator, I went down to Montgomery to help with the work there. I think you probably read about the meeting which took place in the church in Montgomery that night, at which Martin Luther King, the Freedom Riders, and a number of other people were present. When the police would not afford the church protection, a car was burned. There were incidents of violence and a mob of thousands, I understand, gathered outside. People in the church that night didn't know how close they were to real tragedy. This was the night martial law was declared in Montgomery. That night everyone remained in the church throughout the night.

Now something very interesting took place in the church that night. I think it can almost be a generalization that the Negroes in Alabama and Mississippi and elsewhere in the deep South are terribly afraid until they get into the movement. In the dire danger in which we were that night, no one expressed anything except concern for freedom and the thought that someday we'll be free. We stayed there until dawn and everyone was naturally tired, but no one said so. There were about three thousand people there that night, representing all walks of life, from young children to the elder people in the community. I don't think I've ever seen a group of people band together as the crowd in the church did that night.

Finally at dawn, we were escorted home by the troops. The students boarded the bus for Jackson, along with a second bus that had come from Nashville carrying five ministers. The buses left for Jackson, Mississippi, and I think we pretty well know the story from there on. Immediately upon arrival, the people were jailed. Since then there have been roughly three hundred people jailed for doing nothing more than riding a bus.

Shifting the Blame

It interests me that the Freedom Riders have been called "trouble makers," "seekers of violence," and "seekers of publicity." Few people have seen the point: here are people acting within their constitutional and moral rights; they have done nothing more than ride a bus or use a facility that anyone else would normally expect to use any day of the year, but they have been confined and imprisoned for it. And somehow the Attorney General and the President of the United States and the Justice Department of the United States can do nothing about such a gross injustice. As far as being seekers of violence and publicity, the students have, at all times, remained non-violent. Are not the committers of violence responsible for their own actions? . . .

I think that quite often today you can hear the strains of a very old spiritual that's sung quite seriously. Some of the words are: "Before I be a slave I would be buried in my grave and go home to My Lord and be free."

From those who say they approve the ends, not the means, I would be interested in suggestions for a means which would yield freedom without delay. Let us look at the means. The students have chosen non-violence as a technique; there is no reason why they couldn't have taken up guns. It was a responsible choice, I think. We have decided that if there is to be suffering in this revolution (which is really what the movement is—a revolution), we will take the suffering upon ourselves and never inflict it upon our fellow man, because we respect him and recognize the God within him.

The Popular Movement Is a Revolt Against the Black Leadership Class

Louis E. Lomax

In this piece, Louis E. Lomax, a native of Georgia who at the time of writing was a journalist living in New York, considers what he believes is the decline of the black leadership class. According to Lomax, one of the most important aspects of the movement for desegregation is that it was a grassroots movement, conducted by ordinary blacks, especially students. This, he says, is in sharp contrast to civil rights struggles of the past, which tended to rely on established organizations, such as the National Association for the Advancement of Colored People, and well-known black leaders. This emphasis on black leadership, against which Lomax considers the popular movement to be a revolt, was elitist and wrongly bought into white stereotypes about the black masses, Lomax argues. The grassroots movement, instead of focusing attention on key leaders who present themselves as talented beyond the norm, depends on and asserts the worth and dignity of every individual black, Lomax argues. Throughout the South, he believes, black people are stepping out from the shadows of their appointed leaders, and that is a natural step in the movement for independence and equality.

As you read, consider the following questions:
1. Upon what myths does Lomax believe the notion of the "black leadership class" rests?

Excerpted from "The Negro Revolt Against 'The Negro Leaders,'" by Louis E. Lomax, *Harper's Magazine*, June 1960. Copyright © 1960 by *Harper's Magazine*. Reprinted with permission.

2. Why does Lomax think the black leadership class no longer best serves the black cause?
3. To what does Lomax attribute the success of the popular movement?

As Pastor Kelly Miller Smith walked to the lectern to begin his Sunday sermon, he knew his parishioners wanted and needed more than just another spiritual message. The congregation—most of them middle-class Americans, many of them university students and faculty members—sat before him waiting, tense; for Nashville, like some thirty-odd other Southern college towns, on that first Sunday in March of this year, was taut with racial tension in the wake of widespread student demonstrations against lunch-counter discrimination in department stores.

Among the worshipers in Pastor Smith's First Baptist Church were some of the eighty-five students from Fisk and from Tennessee Agricultural and Industrial University who had been arrested and charged with conspiracy to obstruct trade and commerce because they staged protests in several of Nashville's segregated eating places. Just two days before, Nashville police had invaded Mr. Smith's church—which also served as headquarters for the demonstrators—and arrested one of their number, James Lawson, Jr., a Negro senior theological student at predominantly white Vanderbilt University, on the same charge.

The adult members of the congregation were deeply troubled. They knew, as did Negroes all over America, that the spontaneous and uncorrelated student demonstrations were more than an attack on segregation: they were proof that the Negro leadership class, epitomized by the National Association for the Advancement of Colored People, was no longer the prime mover of the Negro's social revolt.

Each protest had a character of its own, tailored to the local goals it sought to achieve. Neither the advice nor the aid of recognized Negro leaders was sought until after the students had set the policy, engaged the enemy, and joined the issue. Despite the probability that the demonstrations would be met with violence, the students took direct action, something Negro leadership organizations consistently counseled against. By forcing these organizations not only to come to their aid but to do their bidding, these militant young people completely reversed the power flow within the Negro community. . . .

The Issue Is Dignity

The demonstrators have shifted the desegregation battle from the courtroom to the market place, and have shifted the main issue to one of individual dignity, rather than civil rights. Not that civil rights are unimportant—but, as these students believe, once the dignity of the Negro individual is admitted, the debate over his right to vote, attend public schools, or hold a job for which he is qualified becomes academic.

Thus, the Negro question, as Tocqueville called it, comes full circle, back to where it started late in the seventeenth century when Christian and puritan America, supported by a good deal of spurious scholarship, downgraded the Negro from villenage (a state he shared with the entire servant class of that era) to slavery, by arguing the inferiority of the Negro as a human being—a soul to be saved, most certainly, but a being somewhat lower than the white Christian with respect to the angels. This concept endured during Reconstruction in the South after the Civil War and formed the foundation upon which the complex and sometimes contradictory structure of segregation was built.

Negro leaders spent seventy-five years remodeling that structure, trying to make it more livable by removing such horrible reminders of the past as lynchings, denial of the ballot, restrictive covenants in housing, and inequalities of public facilities. Only after the intractable Deep South emasculated every move toward equalization did the Negro leadership class sue for school integration. Even then it was a segmented, room-by-room assault. But these student demonstrators have—in effect—put dynamite at the cornerstone of segregation and lit the fuse.

This revolt, swelling under ground for the past two decades [1940–1960], means the end of the traditional Negro leadership class. Local organization leaders were caught flat-footed by the demonstrations; the parade had moved off without them. In a series of almost frantic moves this spring [1960], they lunged to the front and shouted loud, but they were scarcely more than a cheering section— leaders no more. . . .

The Leadership Myth

The NAACP's frank admission that it had no part in planning a demonstration against segregation that resulted in upwards of a thousand Negroes being jailed—coupled with its prompt defense of the demonstrators—marks the end of the great era of the Negro leadership class: a half-century of fiercely guarded glory, climaxed by the historic school desegregation decision of 1954, during which the NAACP by dint of sheer militancy, brains, and a strong moral cause became the undisputed commander-in-chief of the Negro's drive for equality. These demonstrations also ended a two-century-long *modus vivendi* based on the myth of the Negro leader.

The phrase "Negro leadership class" pops up, Minerva-like, in most histories and essays about the Negro. White writers generally take its validity for granted, but Negro writers, of late, when they speak analytically of the Negro leader, do so with contempt.

The myth of a Black Moses, the notion that Negroes had or needed a leader, began to take shape in the early years of the nation when a troubled America viewed the Negro as an amorphous mass undulating in the wilderness of ignorance rather than as individuals, each to be dealt with purely on merit. When the myth took on flesh, the Negro leader had the provincial outlook of the white community that fashioned him: in the pre-Civil War North, Frederick Douglass, leading his people out of slavery; in the South, the plantation preacher.

Had Emancipation meant that the Negro would become

just another of the racial strains to be absorbed into the American melting pot, the myth of the Negro leader would have evaporated. But as Abraham Lincoln so clearly stated, this is precisely what Emancipation did not mean. Consequently, the myth not only continued but took on even greater significance.

There were three chief prerequisites for becoming a Negro leader: (1) approbation of the white community, (2) literacy (real or assumed), and (3) some influence over the Negro masses. Each community spawned an array of "professors," "doctors" (not medical men), "preachers," "bishops," "spokesmen" who sat down at the segregated arbitration table and conducted business in the name of the Negro masses.

These leaders received their credentials and power both from the white community and from the Negro masses, who stood humble before their white-appointed leaders. This status was heady stuff for the early twentieth-century Negro elite, many of whom could remember the snap of the master's whip, and they began to function as a social class. As a result, three generations of educated Negroes dreamed of an equal but separate America in which white power spoke only to black power and black power spoke only to God, if even to Him.

But the Negro leadership class has produced some practical and positive results: the concept provided America with an easy way of doing business with a people it had wronged and did not understand; it provided a platform for talented Negroes—many of whom were dedicated to the interests of the masses. During the last three decades, however, Negro leadership organizations, based in the North and with a national approach to the Negro's problem, eclipsed the local leaders. The heads of these organizations assumed the general title of "Leader of Leaders.". . .

Incomplete Victory

I was there and it was a moving and unforgettable experience to see Negro students at Clinton, Sturgis, Clay, and

Little Rock dodge bricks as they raced to and from school under armed guard. It was a magnificent hour for these fortuitously elite youngsters, many of whom became international heroes. But few of us lost sight of the Negro masses in these cities. They were still called "Jim," "Mary," "Aunt Harriet," and "Uncle Job"; they had to buy clothes they were not allowed to try on; their homes were searched by police without warrants; their heads were bloodied, their jobs threatened if they dared protest. They darted in and out of drug and department stores where they dared not sit down. They were denied free access to the polls, and if they received a just day in court it was usually when all parties concerned were Negroes.

Despite the march of well-scrubbed, carefully selected Negro students into previously all-white schools, it was crystal clear that the fundamental question of the Negro's dignity as an individual had not been resolved. The glory was the NAACP's and nobody begrudged it. Yet, there was a widespread doubt that a nationally directed battle of attrition that took so long and cost so much to bring so little to so few would ever get to the heart of the issue. . . .

An Elitist Group

Meanwhile the Negro leadership class—itself often guilty of rank, class, and color discrimination—was continuing to operate under a concept that begged the question of the dignity of the Negro individual. The literature of Negro progress is littered with such terms as "the talented tenth," "the exceptional Negro," "the new Negro," "the breakthrough Negro," and in recent years "the accepted" and "the assimilated Negro." Sharing the outlook of the white liberals who finance them, and sincerely so, Negro leadership organizations have focused their attention, by and large, on matters that are of interest to the talented Negro rather than the Negro masses. By so doing the Negro leadership class ignored the basic problem of human dignity in favor of themselves and their white peers—a distinction which the segregationists refused to accept. Thus an impassable void has separated the leaders of both sides for the past decade; and the ordinary Negro has been in the no man's land between.

The lunch-counter demonstrations moved to the center of the void, and menaced both principals: the recalcitrant South, by striking closer to the heart of segregation than any other widespread local movements have ever struck before; the Negro leadership class by exposing its impotence.

The Negro leadership class, still torn by jealousy, dissension, and power struggles, rushed to the aid of the students and their mass supporters, and attempted to make complete recovery by "correlating" and "co-ordinating" the movements. But as one Southern NAACP branch president said to me, "how can I correlate something when I don't know where and when it's going to happen?"

I found that established leaders don't have the same fire in their stomachs that the students and the rallying Negro masses have. As the Southern Regional Council interim report on the demonstrations reflects, Southern leaders, Negro and white, are saying, "Before this happened we could have integrated lunch counters. Now it is almost impossible." What the report does not explain is why the lunch counters were not already integrated. This, again, is black power talking to white power about something neither fully understands.

The Genius Behind It
When I talked to the students and their mass supporters I heard them quote the *Wall Street Journal,* of all things, to show that they had hit the segregationists in the pocketbook. I also discovered that in March five Southern cities had already yielded to the demands of the demonstrators and were serving Negroes at lunch counters without incident. Eighteen other cities had interracial committees working to resolve the matter. In each case the students have made it plain that they will not accept segregation in any form.

But neither the students nor their real supporters dwelt

unduly on such practical results. For them, individually and as a group, the victory came when they mustered the courage to look the segregationists in the face and say, "I'm no longer afraid!"

The genius of the demonstrations lies in their spirituality; in their ability to enlist every Negro, from the laborer to the leader, and inspire him to seek suffering as a badge of honor. By employing such valid symbols as singing, praying, reading Gandhi, quoting Thoreau, remembering Martin Luther King, preaching Christ, but most of all by suffering themselves—being hit by baseball bats, kicked, and sent to jail—the students set off an old-fashioned revival that has made integration an article of faith with the Negro masses who, like other masses, are apathetic toward voting and education.

Now the cook, the maid, the butler, and the chauffeur are on fire with the new faith. For the first time since slavery the South is facing a mass revolt against segregation. There is no total explanation for what has happened. All I know is that as I talked with the participants I realized that people were weary of the very fact of segregation. They were no longer content "to let the NAACP do it"; they wanted to get into the fight and they chose the market place, the great center of American egalitarianism, not because it had any overwhelming significance for them but because it was there—accessible and segregated. Tomorrow—and they all believe there will be a tomorrow—their target will be something else.

Few of the masses who have come to the support of these students realize that in attacking segregation under the banner of idealism they are fighting a battle they refused for five years to enter in the name of legalism. But there is a twinkle in the Southern Negro's eye. One gets the feeling that he is proud, now that he has come to full stature and has struck out with one blow against both segregation and the stifling control of Negro leaders.

A Letter from Jail

Patricia Stephens

When she wrote the following letter, Patricia Stephens was a young university student serving a sixty-day sentence for her role in a sit-in protest in Tallahassee, Florida. Such protests were an important part of desegregation efforts, and typically involved young black students sitting peacefully at lunch counters, often for hours on end, waiting for service. The students were trained to be polite and respectful at all times, and to resist the taunts and insults that were often directed against them. For many Americans witnessing these protests on their television screens, the students were models of moral courage, and the peaceful protests helped galvanize public support behind the cause of desegregation. In her letter, which is written in a calm, matter-of-fact tone, Stephens describes how she came to be involved in the protests. She also recounts how she and some of her fellow students, who had been protesting peacefully at a department store lunch counter, were arrested by order of the mayor of Tallahassee. When she was convicted of disturbing the peace and unlawful assembly, Stephens faced either a $300 fine or sixty days in jail. She opted for jail, she writes, because she believed that would best promote the cause of equality.

As you read, consider the following questions:

1. What effect does Stephens create by writing in calm, reserved prose, rather than with emotionally charged language?
2. Why might Stephens think accepting a jail sentence rather than paying a fine would better promote racial equality?

Excerpted from *Freedom Ride*, by James Peck (New York: Simon and Schuster, 1962). Copyright © 1960 by Patricia Stephens. Reprinted with permission of Simon and Schuster.

3. Why doesn't Stephens ever say whether the waitress, the mayor, the policemen, the judge, and the guards in her story are white or black?

I am writing this in Leon County Jail. My sister Priscilla and I, five other A & M [Florida Agricultural and Mechanical University] students, and one high school student are serving sixty-day sentences for our participation in the sit-ins. We could be out on appeal but we all strongly believe that Martin Luther King was right when he said, "We've got to fill the jails in order to win our equal rights." Priscilla and I both explained this to our parents when they visited us the other day. Priscilla is supposed to be on a special diet and mother was worried about her. We did our best to dispel her worries. We made it clear that we want to serve out our full time.

Students who saw the inside of the county jail before I did, and were released on bond, reported that conditions were miserable. They did not exaggerate. It is dank and cold. We are in what is called a "bull tank" with four cells. Each cell has four bunks, a commode, and a small sink. Some of the cells have running water, but ours does not. Breakfast, if you can call it that, is served at six-thirty. Another meal is served at twelve-thirty and in the evening, "sweet" bread and watery coffee. At first I found it difficult to eat this food. Two ministers visit us every day. Sundays and Wednesdays are regular visiting days, but our white visitors who came at first are no longer permitted by the authorities.

There is plenty of time to think in jail and I sometimes review in my mind the events which brought me here. It is almost six months since Priscilla and I were first introduced to CORE [Congress of Racial Equality] at a workshop in Miami. Upon our return we helped to establish a Tallahassee CORE group, whose initial meeting took place last October [1959]. Among our first projects was a test sit-in at Sears' and McCrory's. So, we were not totally unprepared when the South-wide protest movement started in early February.

An Inside View

Our first action in Tallahassee was on February 13. At eleven A.M. we sat down at the Woolworth lunch counter. When the waitress approached, Charles Steele, who was next to me, ordered a slice of cake for each of us. She said, "I'm sorry. I can't serve you," and moved on down the counter, repeating this to the other participants. We all said we would wait, took out our books, and started reading— or at least, we tried.

The regular customers continued to eat. When one man finished, the waitress said, "Thank you for staying and eating in all this indecency." The man replied, "What did you expect me to do? I paid for it."

One man stopped behind Bill Carpenter briefly and said, "I think you're doing a fine job. Just sit right there." A young white hoodlum then came up behind Bill and tried to bait him into an argument. Unsuccessful, he boasted to his friends, "I bet if I disjoint him, he'll talk." When Bill didn't respond, he moved on. A number of tough-looking characters wandered into the store. In most instances the waitress spotted them and had them leave. When a few of them started making derisive comments, the waitress said about us, "You can see they aren't here to start anything." Although the counters were closed twenty minutes after our arrival, we stayed until two P.M.

The second sit-in at Woolworth's occurred a week later. The waitress saw us sitting down and said, "Oh Lord, here they come again!" This time a few white persons were participating secretly. They simply sat and continued eating without comment. The idea was to demonstrate the reality of eating together without coercion, contamination, or cohabitation. Everything was peaceful. We read. I was reading the *Blue Book of Crime* and Barbara Broxton, *How to Tell the Different Kinds of Fingerprints*—which gave us a laugh in light of the arrests which followed.

At about three-thirty P.M. a squad of policemen led by a man in civilian clothes entered the store. Someone directed him to Priscilla, who had been chosen our spokesman for this sit-in. "As Mayor of Tallahassee, I am asking you to leave," said the man in civilian clothes.

"If we don't leave, would we be committing a crime?" Priscilla asked. The mayor simply repeated his original statement. Then he came over to me, pointed to the "closed" sign, and asked, "Can you read?" I advised him to direct all his comments to our elected spokesman. He looked as though his official vanity was wounded but turned to Priscilla. We did too, reiterating our determination to stay. He ordered our arrest.

Two policemen "escorted" each of the eleven of us to the station. I use quotes because their handling of us was not exactly gentle nor were their remarks courteous. At four forty-five we entered the police station. Until recently the building had housed a savings and loan company, so I was not surprised to observe that our cell was a renovated bank vault. One by one, we were fingerprinted.

After about two hours, the charges against us were read and one of us was allowed to make a phone call. I started to call Reverend C. K. Steele, a leader of nonviolent action in Tallahassee whose two sons were involved in the sit-ins. A policeman stopped me on the grounds that Reverend Steele is not a bondsman. I heard a number of policemen refer to us as "niggers" and say we should stay on the campus.

Shortly, the police captain came into our cell and announced that someone was coming to get us out. An hour later we were released—through the back door, so that the waiting reporters and TV men would not see us and give us publicity. However, the reporters were quick to catch on and they circled the building to meet us.

A Vote of Support

We were arraigned February 22 and charged with disturbing the peace by riotous conduct and unlawful assembly. We all pleaded not guilty. The trial was set for March 3. A week prior to the date the entire A & M student body met and decided to suspend classes on March 3 and attend the trial. The prospect of having three thousand students converge on the small courtroom was a factor, we believe, in causing a two-week postponement.

Our biggest single demonstration took place on March 12 at nine A.M. The plan was for Florida State University students, who are white, to enter the two stores first and order food. A & M students would arrive later and, if refused service, would share the food which the white students had ordered. It was decided that I should be an observer this time rather than a participant because of my previous arrest.

The white and Negro students were sitting peacefully at the counter when the mayor and his corps arrived. As on the previous occasion, he asked the group to leave, but when a few rose to comply, he immediately arrested them. As a symbolic gesture of contempt, they were marched to the station in interracial pairs.

After the arrests many of us stood in a park opposite the station. We were refused permission to visit those arrested. I rushed back to report this on campus. When I returned to the station, some two hundred students were with me. Barbara Cooper and I, again, asked to visit those arrested. Again, we were refused.

A Close Call

Thereupon, we formed two groups and headed for the variety stores. The seventeen who went to McCrory's were promptly arrested. The group headed for Woolworth's was met by a band of white hoodlums armed with bats, sticks, knives, and other weapons. They were followed by police. To avoid what seemed certain violence, the group called off the sit-in at Woolworth's and returned to the campus in an orderly manner.

We asked the president of the student body to mobilize the students for a peaceful march downtown. He agreed but first tried, without success, to arrange a conference with the mayor.

However, the mayor was not too busy to direct the city,

county, and state police who met us as we neared the downtown area. There were one thousand of us, in groups of seventy-five—each with two leaders. Our hastily printed posters said: "Give Us Our Students Back," "We Will Not Fight Mobs," "No Violence," "We Want Our Rights: We are Americans, Too."

As we reached the police line-up, the mayor stepped forward and ordered us to disperse within three minutes. But the police did not wait. They started shooting tear gas bombs at once. One policeman, turning on me, exclaimed, "I want you!" and thereupon aimed one of the bombs directly at me.

The students moved back toward campus. Several girls were taken to the university hospital to be treated for burns. Six students were arrested, bringing the total arrests for the day to thirty-five. Bond was set at five hundred dollars each and within two days all were out.

The eleven of us arrested on February 20 were tried on March 17. There was no second postponement. The trial started promptly at nine-thirty. Five additional charges had been made against us, but were subsequently dropped. During the trial, Judge Rudd tried to keep race out of the case. He said it was not a factor in our arrest. But we realized it was the sole factor. The mayor in his testimony used the word "nigger" freely. We were convicted and sentenced to sixty days in jail or a three-hundred-dollar fine. All eleven had agreed to go to jail but three paid fines upon advice of our attorneys.

So, here I am serving a sixty-day sentence along with seven other CORE members. When I get out, I plan to carry on this struggle. I feel I shall be ready to go to jail again if necessary.

Do Nonviolent Protesters Try to Provoke Violence?

Jan Howard

In this selection, Jan Howard, who was active in the struggle for desegregation, discusses the much touted tactic of nonviolent protest. According to Howard, although those staging such protests were usually openly committed to shunning violence, the protests themselves often relied on the provocation of violence. Nonviolent protests tended to work, Howard says, only when racist whites responded violently to peaceful black protesters because only then would the broader public, appalled at the violence, give their support to the blacks. In this way, she argues, nonviolent protesters, even though they themselves were not violent, relied on the violence of white racists. Furthermore, Howard says, when such violence was not forthcoming, the protesters felt their efforts were futile, and were unable to capture the attention they desired. Howard also argues that a tension within groups fighting segregation, between those who favored nonviolence, and those eager to use violence, helped push civil rights leaders toward relying on retaliatory violence. Howard ends her piece with the worry that civil rights groups might turn overtly to violence, which is indeed what happened in the years following the publication of her piece, as the movement shifted from the South, where the violence of white racists was easily provoked, to the North, where black activists were largely ignored rather than attacked.

As you read, consider the following questions:
1. What does Howard think would have happened if nonviolent protests had not provoked violence by racist whites?
2. Why does Howard think violence was necessary?
3. How does Howard implicitly define violence? Is it the mere use of force, or is it something more than that? For instance, does she consider being arrested, or having police block one's way, to be a form of violence?

The civil rights movement is pledged to nonviolence. It is commonly assumed by those of us involved in it that the provocation of violence is alien to its strategy and that violence is simply a calculated risk in trying to achieve its goals. But the facts compel me to question this assumption and to suggest that the provocation of violence is often used as a latent tactic.

This contention is difficult to prove. I am certain many of us working for civil rights are unconscious of the way we exploit violence. And since the whole ideology of the movement implies an abhorrence of violence, none of us wants to admit that violence is more than a calculated risk. In the South violence against civil rights workers often occurs spontaneously, without any attempt to invite it; so it is hard to know where provocation as risk leaves off and provocation as tactic begins.

Violence as a Strategy

Yet, the record suggests that in many situations the provocation of violence has become more than a calculated risk of the movement. It has the earmarks of a strategy.

Consider what happened in the 1964 Mississippi Summer Project. Its purposes were to register Negroes to vote; to teach them in Freedom Schools; and to expose white college students to the rigors of Southern poverty and repression. I understand still another goal was expressed by leaders of the project long before it actually began—getting federal troops to Mississippi to protect the voter registration drive. The fulfillment of this goal hinged on violence, and the leaders knew it. They also knew something else—that the government was reluctant to provide protection. For several years a seasoned cadre of Negro civil rights workers had been waging the voter registration drive under conditions of open brutality and terror. When they asked for federal protection, the government was uncooperative.

Leaders of the movement anticipated that bringing hundreds of outsiders to Mississippi would trigger violence, but this time the violence would be against students from white, affluent, influential families, and the federal government would be forced to protect them. The prophecy was largely correct. The project had only begun when three of the workers were murdered. This single act gave the program more publicity than any other kind of action could have. It did not bring federal troops, but it brought FBI agents and federal marshals in large numbers, and by their presence they reduced the likelihood of violence against the civil rights workers.

Relying on Violence

The chain of events in this and similar situations forces us to consider this question: when is the provocation of violence more than a calculated risk of the movement? I suggest an answer: when the movement adopts a goal which it believes can be fulfilled only through violence. It is then, in effect, relying on violence to achieve some end. Violence is not simply a calculated risk; it is part of an over-all plan. And the instrumental value of violence is a built-in impetus for actions that will provide it.

Because the Summer Project had so many goals, one can always argue that the goal of getting federal troops had no special effect on the actions of the movement. It would have brought the students South anyway. This argument begs the question. With respect to achieving one goal, the provocation of violence can be merely a calculated risk; but with respect to achieving another, it can be a latent tactic.

Selma, Alabama, provides another illustration of what I have in mind. In discussing the rationale behind the Selma protest, Dr. Martin Luther King clearly suggests that the movement in Selma, like the movement in Mississippi, was relying on violence to achieve some goal.

> The goal of the demonstrations in Selma, as elsewhere, is to dramatize the existence of injustice and to bring about the presence of justice. . . . Long years of experience indicate to us that Negroes can achieve this goal when four things occur:
> 1. Nonviolent demonstrators go into the streets to exercise their constitutional rights.
> 2. *Racists resist by unleashing violence against them.*
> 3. Americans of conscience in the name of decency demand federal intervention and legislation.
> 4. The Administration, under mass pressure, initiates measures of immediate intervention and remedial legislation.

When nonviolent protest does provoke violent retaliation, civil rights leaders know how to capitalize on the situation and turn it to our advantage. But when nonviolence begets nonviolent opposition, this can really frustrate the movement, as I learned firsthand at Selma in the days immediately following the march that turned around. The police then blocked us from marching to the county courthouse. And King's aides followed his example, leading us to the barricades but no further.

A Sense of Failure

We were gripped by a tremendous sense of frustration and futility. I believe this reaction was caused in large part by the failure of the nonviolent technique to provoke violence. Safety Director Baker headed the police, and they were on their best behavior. They refused to be provoked into violence even when a group of Negro youths broke ranks and charged their line, and Baker readily approved all forms of nonviolent protest such as speeches and prayers. Thus, demonstrators found it impossible to make the police initiate action that the movement could capitalize on. We were forced either to be violent ourselves or to bear the burden of seemingly ineffective nonviolence. And for many this burden was shame—shame because we were just standing there, not getting through, not pushing through, not being beaten, not being arrested, just standing there.

The obvious sign of failure was that we were not getting through to the courthouse. But I think participants also sensed a more subtle sign of failure: the lack of violence. When you turn the other cheek and nobody bothers to slap it, it's hard to believe you are a threat to anyone. Both kinds of failure were articulated by spokesmen for the movement when they announced on the evening of the all-night vigil: "We will tell the police: You must let us through, or you must beat us, tear gas us, or jail us." In essence they were imploring: "You must let nonviolence work, or you must be violent. Give us some sense of effectiveness."

Why Violence Works

I am not suggesting participants in the movement are attracted to violence for its own sake. But I am suggesting we are consciously and unconsciously drawn toward violence because violence pays dividends for the movement.

First and foremost, it is a powerful catalyst to arouse public opinion. If the 600 Negroes who were tear gassed and beaten in Selma had walked all the way to Montgomery without a violent incident, we would still be awaiting a voting bill. Nor is Selma an isolated case. It was the bombings in Birmingham that forced President Kennedy to submit the historic Civil Rights Bill. The bared fangs of Bull Connor's police dogs—the burning bus of the Freedom Riders—the tear-stained face of Medgar Evers' widow: these are the alarms that awaken the conscience of America.

When bigotry erupts into violence, this dramatizes the everyday plight of the Negro and shows the righteousness of the movement's cause. In the words of Dr. King, the murder of the three civil rights workers was "a grisly and eloquent demonstration to the whole nation of the moral degeneracy upon which segregation rests." Can nonviolence pay such "eloquent" dividends?

Violence is dramatic, and Americans like the dramatic. Mass media will give extensive coverage to violence and threats of violence while they ignore more subtle injustices against the Negro and more subtle attempts to remedy injustice. And the federal government can be forced to intervene in situations of violence while it turns its back on less inflammatory brutality.

Playing to the Audience

But there is more to the attraction of violence than its power to arouse the public at large. Civil rights leaders have other audiences in mind when they march into battle. They are trying to arouse the apathetic Negro by showing him that other Negroes would rather stand up in battle than be bent by the yoke of submission. And they are trying to bolster the nerve of the active Negro as well. To quote Dr. King:

> Those who have lived under the corrosive humiliation of daily intimidation are imbued by demonstrations with a sense of courage and dignity that strengthens their personalities. Through demonstrations, Negroes learn that unity and militance have more force than bullets. They find that the bruises of clubs, electric cattle prods and fists hurt less than the scars of submission.

The enemy constitutes still another audience. According to King, "segregationists learn from demonstrations that Negroes who have been taught to fear can also be taught to be fearless."

A further attraction of violence for participants in a nonviolent movement inheres in the fact that violence is the antithesis of nonviolence. Thus, the moral superiority of nonviolence is most graphically displayed in a violent setting.

Nonviolence reaches the height of its legitimacy when it is counterposed with the illegitimacy of naked violence.

Finally, we should recognize that not all participants in the movement are philosophically committed to nonviolence. There is division in the ranks, and this is another pressure toward violence. A sizable number scattered throughout the movement do not believe in nonviolence, either as a principle or a tactic. Even the group that subscribes to nonviolence is divided. Some are committed to it as an end in itself; others view it simply as an expedient tactic. Since the latter have no philosophical attachment to nonviolence, they are more vulnerable to the appeal of violence as a strategy than the committed are. This group and the nonbelievers are constantly pressuring the committed to prove that nonviolence works. Sometimes this pressure forces the committed to exploit violence as a means of gaining symbolic victories for nonviolence. They may hastily involve the movement in a dramatic protest because they know drama has a quick pay-off. Or they may try other means of winning laurels for nonviolence even if they have to throw caution and some principles to the winds. As they are forced to take more and more chances, violence as risk becomes violence as certainty.

I felt the pressure on the leaders in Selma when nonviolence appeared to be ineffective. The situation was so tense and the youngsters were so eager to take on the police that King's aides had to respond to the dissatisfaction. They made several frantic attempts to show that nonviolence works. On at least two occasions they sent small groups to the courthouse by evasive routes to stage a demonstration. One venture came within a hair of triggering mob violence. But the leaders could say to their critics that they had succeeded in getting past the police nonviolently.

Not Always Effective

I am not suggesting that the violence of white segregationists always pays dividends for the movement. The impact on the public at large depends in part on the character of the victim. The brutalizing of whites arouses much more attention and anger than the brutalizing of Negroes. Violence which rallies national sentiment behind the movement can tear a local community apart and freeze positions, so that it becomes more difficult to win localized demands. Even on a national level, a given type of violence seems to pay diminishing returns. Tear gas in Selma outraged the nation, but only three weeks later smoke bombs in Camden went practically unnoticed. Does the American public have a rising degree of tolerance for violence? If so, there must be an escalation of violence to get the same effect. This may be an unforeseen consequence of using the dramatic protest to arouse public opinion.

The strategy of the movement in this country raises a very important question: Does a movement which is dedicated to nonviolence as *the* means of action and reaction inherently need violence to sustain it? The evidence suggests that it does. I remember what Reverend Andrew Young, one of King's top aides, said in Browns Chapel as he reflected on the fact that Safety Director Baker was a nonviolent police chief. He said that the Bakers really thwart the movement but that the Bull Connors and Jim Clarks play into its hands and give it momentum.

The philosophy of nonviolent struggle seems in part to be predicated on the idea that there will be violence against the movement. The success of nonviolent struggle may require that this prophecy be fulfilled. Thus, we who are involved may be captives of a social dynamic, without necessarily being aware of the forces acting upon us. I still hear the words of the parade captain I spoke to in the march that turned around. As we followed the leaders back to Selma, he vociferously declared:

"We should have kept marching
right through the troopers!"
"And what price are you willing
to pay to keep marching?" I asked.
"One life? Ten lives? A hundred?"
"No lives," he replied. "No lives."

Did he really mean "no lives"? Or was he refusing to admit even to himself that the nonviolent movement often thrives on violence? Perhaps he was refusing to admit something even more important—that he is disillusioned with the nonviolent approach to winning battles.

The violence of white segregationists may be necessary to sustain the nonviolent movement, but it may not be sufficient. If the public and the government do not respond to that violence, and what it represents, with enough indignation and power to change the Negro's inhuman condition to a human one—then the Negro and his white allies will totally abandon nonviolence as a principle and strategy. Already we see the emergence of the Deacons, an armed league of Negroes pledged to using violence in self-defense. And we see the nonviolent movement wrestling with its conscience and struggling to cope with the attitudes represented by the Deacons. Pressured by the reality of life, the movement has already embraced the tactic of capitalizing on violence and the tactic of provoking it. To sustain itself, will it now be forced to sanction the use of violence in self-defense? What is the next step?

The Perspective of the Ordinary White

Robert Coles

Although protesting blacks and angry, violent whites captured most of the headlines during the desegregation movement, many blacks and whites in the South, perhaps even most, didn't fit into either category. In the following piece, Robert Coles discusses the Southerners who were neither actively promoting nor strenuously resisting desegregation. Coles discusses a white shopkeeper in Georgia whom he came to know well, who professed to maintain a segregated store for basic economic reasons, and who didn't see himself as being responsible for a complex structure that oppressed blacks. Coles traces the development of the attitudes of this shopkeeper, who presumably represents many white Southerners, as the protests at his store progressed, through to its eventual integration in 1965. Coles, the author of over fifty books, is a Harvard professor and a child psychiatrist. As Scott London, a journalist, characterized Coles's approach as an author, "Coles's technique is to get to know children, students, volunteer workers, etc., ask them significant questions, and simply let them speak. He strongly believes that people's stories speak for themselves."

As you read, consider the following questions:
1. Why does the shopkeeper believe that he is not responsible for segregation?
2. The author, Robert Coles, never expresses his own opinion of racial segregation. What effect does this have on the reader?
3. How might this piece be different if the author were black?

Excerpted from *Children of Crisis: A Study of Courage and Fear*, by Robert Coles (Boston, MA: Little, Brown, and Company, 1964). Copyright © 1964 by Robert Coles. Reprinted with permission.

Even when an entire social system is in convulsive transition there are many who neither try hard to resist change nor lift a willing finger to bring about a new kind of life. From people on both sides of the struggle one hears summoned the "ordinary" man, the "average guy," the "typical person" as potentially friendly, vaguely supportive, fitfully antagonistic, or somewhat—but only somewhat—alarmed. Such descriptions, inevitably tentative, ambiguous or openended, reflect the uneasy truth known to ideologues and just plain idealists of all persuasions: many people, perhaps most people, are content to live in society rather than commit themselves to its alteration, let alone transformation. Among those so content are numbered the discontented as well as the reasonably well-to-do. Just as I have found all classes represented in both the sit-in movement and the various segregationist organizations, I have found among a wide range of people in both races an essential determination that their lives—in the words of one (Negro) citizen of Georgia—"not be bothered by all the trouble around."

The more I watched sit-ins and other demonstrations over the South the more interested I became in the specific psychological effect they exerted. What happened to white people (or Negroes) as youths or ministers quietly, solemnly marched before them, or toward them? During a long—perhaps too long—interview with a tired, angry, still nonviolent Negro youth in Atlanta I heard him suggest an end to our talks, and a beginning for another series of conversations.

Minding One's Own Business

"I can see how you might want to know how someone like me keeps his head from splitting in all directions, but I think you're losing a real opportunity. You should go speak with those white folks—the ones who look at us, and stare, just stare without giving a clue what's going on in their minds. Or you could go talk to the store owners we picket. Some of them look as if they're ready to go mad, not get mad. One came out yesterday and begged us to leave him alone. He said he didn't care one way or the other what happened. He just wanted to make a living and mind his own business—I mean *really* mind his own business, without us bothering him. We told him he could. All we wanted was to help him make *more* money, by serving us. But no. He said the white people would stop coming, and he'd go broke or have to move to a Negro neighborhood.

"To tell the truth, I felt sorry for the guy. I don't know how he feels about segregation and integration, but he didn't strike me as very different from my own parents. They want to stay alive, and when given half a chance, they'll keep quiet and do just that, stay alive. Now the trouble is, a lot more Negroes have trouble staying alive than whites, so a lot more of us are moved—moved to *do* something, get involved in the *movement*. But there are plenty of Negroes, even the poorest—maybe especially the poorest in some towns—who don't want to get involved. They say leave me alone, and after you've tried to get them to join you, and they've said leave me alone again, only louder, you know they mean it."

I went to talk with the very storekeeper he mentioned, and eventually came to know him rather well. The Negro student knew him only as a demonstrator does a man of property who repeatedly refuses what is asked of him. I soon learned, however, that the nonviolent student was a shrewd—and in a way compassionate—judge of human nature. Eventually I was able to tell the middle-aged merchant how the Negro youth had appraised his position and his attitude.

Peace and Quiet

"He's right. I want peace and quiet, and I want to go on making a living. If he knows that, he knows that he's wasting his time trying to preach to me or demonstrate. The way I see it, he and I are together. Neither one of us made the world the way it is; and all I want is to stay alive in it, just as he does. At the rate he's going, he'll spend most of his life in jail, and I'll go broke. What does *that* solve for either of us?"

I found him to be a stubborn but pleasant man, a native-born Georgian, in turn a high school graduate, a soldier in the Second World War, and the recipient of a degree in pharmacy. He bought his drugstore with a large loan, and worked for years to own, really own, his business, located in a small town that is really a suburb of Atlanta.

He and his wife grew up together, and fitted together very well. He tended to be serious, even somber. She had a light touch to her voice and her everyday mood. He worried about money and the marks each of their three children brought home from school. She was a devout Baptist and *believed* in faith: "I tell my husband and my children both that it matters not what things of this world we have, so long as we pray for God's grace." (She would often exalt her sentence structure when reproving what she called "the excessive worldliness about us.") They received me cordially into their home, and talked as openly with me—I became convinced—as they did with their neighbors or, for that matter, between themselves.

Sometimes, particularly when under pressure, her husband fell back upon her outlook. Indeed, one day I heard him, and not her, talk of God with such feeling that I at once sensed I was hearing not only his strongly held opinion but perhaps the (hitherto secret) inspiration for his wife's piety.

Enduring the Protests

"Who ever stops to figure out why we live the way we do? Those nigra students come and try to talk with me and the other businessmen on the block. They tell us they're going to sit in, they're going to picket, they're going to do this and that to embarrass us, and shame us, and make us lose money, until finally we surrender to them. They ask me: don't you feel guilty, don't you feel ashamed for all you've done, all your people have done to us? They say if I don't give in, they'll *make* me—by marching up and down, and being nonviolent, and letting people spit on them, and shout at them, or getting the police to arrest them.

"For a long time I tried to ignore them. First I thought they would get tired and go away; then I thought the police would take care of them, or my customers. But they didn't get tired, and it seems that the more they're arrested, the more they want to come back.

"My customers were the ones that became tired. They told me they just couldn't keep on coming in and out of the store, past those nigra students, with their signs and their songs and their slogans. Some of them made a point of shopping downtown, though the drugstores and restaurants there are being picketed, too. Some tried to cut down on their shopping trips. They would save up things to buy, and come here once instead of twice a week.

"I had to close the counter. Who wants to eat with those people trying to move in and eat beside you? I lost money that way, but there wasn't any choice. Every customer I had would have left me if I hadn't done it. White people won't eat with nigras, and the sooner those students find that out, the better it will be for everyone."

I asked him at that time what he felt about the students. Did they bother him as little as he had been saying, or was he trying to "forget"—at least in our conversations—how troublesome they actually were to him?

Yes, it was true they bothered him, though he wanted very much not to take their actions personally. That was the clue to survival, he felt: "I've seen other businessmen knuckle under. They get so angry at the nigras that they close their stores or they start fighting them, and make all their white customers afraid to come near, for fear of violence. Or they try to make a settlement with the nigras, and lose all their white customers that way."

Live and Let Live
Why did those customers leave—out of fear, distaste, outrage, resentment, shame? Again and again we came back to that issue; he was obviously interested in discussing it, and

I felt that the more he talked about his "average" customer, the more I came to know the contradictory substance of *his* views, not to mention the customer's. They were earnestly held views, but easily abandoned ones. Over several years I watched a changing social and political situation utterly undermine some of those views, and make others seem antique or irrelevant even to the man who once proclaimed them. Yet again and again he did come back to certain principles that *were* consistent.

"Say what you will, people run a store to make money. You offer things to the customers, and you hope they'll buy what you have to sell. Now this race thing has suddenly come up; I don't know from where. All my life I've lived with nigras, and not treated them bad, nor them me bad. We've got along—and recently a lot of them have come to me and told me how sorry they are for what I've gone through. Like with most white folks, a lot of the colored just want to live and let live.

"That's my philosophy: live and let live. You can't make a rich man the equal of a poor man. Even in Russia that guy Khrushchev has villas and big cars and all that, while the peasants live the way our tenant farmers do, or worse. The same holds with race. The white man is different from the nigra, all over the world he is. They say we in the South are unfair to colored people. All I want to know is where do they really give a nigra the same acceptance a white man gets? In Boston, or New York? In England? (I've been reading how they have their problems there, the same ones we do.)

"You go into a nigra's home in Atlanta and you'll see them eating well, and wearing good clothes. They have cars, bigger ones than I would ever buy. They have radio and television, and everything else. I've seen their drugstores. They sell the same things I do. They have what the country has to offer. Isn't that enough?

Just an Ordinary Person

"They try to tell me no—that they're treated inferior. They try to make me feel as if I'm persecuting them, as though

I've done something wrong to hurt them. One of them said to me the other day: 'Don't you feel that in turning us away you're being un-Christian?'

"I say no to them every time. I don't see what Christianity has to do with politics or the customs we have. I don't want to hurt them, and I don't want them to hurt me. It's as simple as that. They're trying to make me into a slave owner, or something. I can see that, and I told them that once. I told them they weren't going to get me angry or excited, the way some people get. They want that to happen. It gives them satisfaction. It makes them think that they're right—that we'll lose control and give in after a while.

"I went to see my minister and talked with him about this. He said that I had to examine my conscience and pray. I told him I have, and that I can't see why I should have to make up for whatever troubles the colored man has in Georgia. I'm just an ordinary person. I can barely depend on enough money to pay my bills. I can't subsidize an integrated cafeteria in my drugstore. Soon it will be segregated again—all black.

"The minister told me that the problem was larger than both of us. (Our church has no colored in it.) He said we both faced a lot of trouble these coming years, through no fault of our own, but because the society is changing and the average man has to adjust himself to it. I told him I was as flexible as anyone—I'm just waiting to see every other drugstore—and church—in Georgia 'adjust.'"

A year later (1963) he was no longer the besieged storekeeper. He had won his battle, and kept his store white. The Negroes eventually tired of demonstrating in front of his store. He continued to fear their renewed interest and attention, and out of his experience he developed an interest in what they were doing elsewhere. He often talked with his customers—and his minister—about "the problem."

"You know, it is our number-one problem today, *the problem*. I'm like you—I have to be in my business. I want to know what people think, where they're headed in their thinking. To be truthful, I think we're slowly going to settle this thing. We already have nigra children in the schools, and it's only a matter of time before they'll be back here asking me for coffee and Cokes. I ask some of my customers what they think, and I can hear them being as annoyed with the whole thing as I am. They're no longer as shocked though—any more than I am. When those colored boys first came here last year I thought they were crazy. Then I thought they were hoodlums pretending to be nice and Christianlike. Now, from what I see on television, they're the younger generation of nigras, or at least they're *some* of the younger generation. I still think a lot of nigras don't care one way or the other. Like most of us whites, they want calm. You only live once, and you don't want to spend your days fighting."

Adjusting to Change

His drugstore was desegregated in 1965, after the Civil Rights Bill was passed. He was nervous and fearful when it happened, but also relieved: "They finally got around to me. To tell the truth, I thought they were overlooking me as not worth their while. I told my wife I felt hurt. When I saw them come in I shuddered again, just like before. They weren't the same nigras, and I thought they might get tough or violent. But they didn't. They just moved in on those counter chairs and asked for coffee. My countergirl looked scared, and confused. She turned to me and asked me with a look what she should do. I didn't say a word. I just nodded to her. She knew what I meant. She started pouring. They didn't seem to want to stay long. They drank a bit, then they got up and left. The three white people at the counter just sat there. They had stopped drinking *their* coffee out of curiosity. We all looked at one another, then one of the customers said to me: 'A store is a store, I guess; and you have to serve whatever walks in from the street.'

"That wasn't the way he talked last year, I remember. But I guess it wasn't the way I did either. It's changing down here, that's what's happening, and the man in the street, he has to keep up with it, even if he doesn't always go along with it. I suppose that comes later, agreeing with what's already happened. Some of my friends say that if we had fought this battle harder, the integration people never would have won. I tell them that we did fight once, and lost. No one ever let us vote on this. We're all segregationists, the white people of Georgia; or most of us are. But we've got caught up in something that's bigger than us, and we've got to live with it, the way I see it. There's no choice. When I say that to them, they agree with me, no matter how much they talk of killing every nigger in sight. So I guess most people make their peace with things as they are."

4

DESEGREGATION IN THE NORTH

CHAPTER PREFACE

For most Americans, segregation was a phenomenon of the South, where the legacy of slavery was strongest and where an elaborate set of statute laws enforced racial separation. But there was another kind of segregation in America, as most whites in the South were eager to point out to their counterparts in the North. Above the Mason-Dixon Line it was usually no less true that whites and blacks lived in different parts of town, attended different schools, and worked in different careers. Whereas in the South segregation was de jure, or legally mandated, in the North segregation was de facto, a fact of life having to do with custom and practice. Although the northern states had abolished slavery long before the southern states had, discriminatory practices remained common. Furthermore, during the first few decades of the twentieth century, huge numbers of blacks migrated from the South to the North, partly to escape the severer abuses of racism and partly to seek economic opportunities in the more highly industrialized North. This migration led to the establishment of expansive black communities in most northern cities, especially in New York, Chicago, Buffalo, and Philadelphia. In this chapter, James Peck argues that blacks in northern cities were not immune to the sting of racism, and he points to the difficulty, and even danger, that many blacks faced in integrating white neighborhoods in the North.

Around 1965, civil rights activists began to turn their attention from the South to the North, focusing not on legal segregation but on the deeply entrenched attitudes and customs that kept the North racially segregated. Although most whites in the North had supported desegregation when the front lines of the battle were in the South, their attitudes were more ambivalent when the segregation concerned was their own. Martin Luther King Jr., for instance, found that it was much harder to confront racism and discrimination in the North, where it was more subtle, more complicated, and cloaked in habit rather than law. Furthermore, when segregation was a matter of habit rather than law, not everyone agreed that it was unjust or thought that governments should actively work to minimize it. The Black Power movement, for instance, which emphasized the development of racial pride among African Americans, did not think that full integration in white society was desirable. James Farmer argues that blacks who were successful at integrating into white communities in the North often felt as if they were traitors to their race, having abandoned black community and culture in favor of assimilation. According to Farmer, full integration may not be as valuable as many blacks had long thought it to be, and he suggests that the black cause could best be served by voluntary segregation, in which blacks, rather than being forced to live apart from whites, chose to cherish and assert their own culture.

One of the most controversial aspects of desegregation in the North was court-ordered busing. In a series of judgments designed to ensure integration despite residential segregation, the courts ordered the development of plans to bus children from white neighborhoods to schools in black communities, and children from black neighborhoods to schools in white communities. Such plans drew strident reactions from parents, especially white parents, in most cities in which they were implemented. An article from *Time* magazine discusses the outbreak of violence in Boston and attributes it to white racism. As the magazine points out, Boston, the birthplace of the Republic, was long considered a place of enlightened liberalism. A different view on the resistance to busing is expressed by the magazine the *New Republic*. In a carefully argued editorial, the magazine insists that, although legally enforced segregation is clearly wrong, it is not clear whether de facto segregation is inherently wrong. Furthermore, it finds that busing is unwise because it fractures communities and encourages disgruntled white parents to enroll their children in private schools, which ultimately leads to a decline in the quality of the public school system on which most blacks depend. For the editorial writer of the *New Republic,* the goal that matters is quality education for everyone, rather than integrated schools at any cost.

Segregation Exists in the North, Too

James Peck

Although segregation in the South attracted the most attention, most communities in the North were segregated too. The segregation in the South was enforced by law, and is thus known as de jure segregation. In the North, where no laws existed enforcing racial separation, segregation was de facto, a simple fact of life that had to do with socioeconomic factors and, more controversially, racism. The following piece, written by James Peck, a noted civil rights activist, discusses one black family's attempt to move into a white neighborhood not far from New York City. According to Peck, the black family moved out of the neighborhood because of threats and intimidation, and Peck reveals that in interviews with white residents, more than one-half didn't want the black family in their neighborhood. Peck's article, which appeared in *The Crisis*, the newsletter of the National Association for the Advancement of Colored People, was published in 1954, the same year the Supreme Court struck down de jure segregation in the South.

As you read, consider the following questions:
1. What are the different reasons offered by those who didn't want the black family to move into the neighborhood?
2. What criticism does Peck levy against the media?
3. Why, given what Peck has said, might there have been reason to think that integration was more promising in the North than in the South?

How prejudiced are residents of a lily-white housing development where a Negro businessman built a home which was twice set afire during the period of construction, received anonymous threatening notes signed Ku Klux Klan, had his fire insurance policy canceled, and finally sold out in order not to submit his three children to an atmosphere of intolerance?

Instead of giving the answer myself, I will leave it to you readers to decide. I will give you direct quotes from the residents of this community as I got them in two house-to-house opinion polls in which I took part—one for the Columbia Broadcasting System, which used the material in a special program about the Negro in America; the other for the New York Committee of Racial Equality.

The Negro businessman involved is Clarence Wilson. I will not go further than I did in the first paragraph to give details about the fires, since they have already been widely publicized in the Negro press as well as by the NAACP [The National Association for the Advancement of Colored People] and other race relations organizations.

The housing development in which Wilson built his house is Deauville Gardens, located near the village of Copiague, on the outskirts of the town of Amityville, Long Island, about 50 miles from New York City. Amityville has a jimcrow section which is ordinarily called North Amityville, but which the more extreme white-supremacy elements call South Farmingdale or West Babylon in an attempt to disassociate it completely from Amityville and to identify it instead with the neighboring towns.

For Whites Only

As for Deauville Gardens, the man after whom it was named left a will stipulating that the land should forever remain in the hands of white Caucasians. Its legal validity has of course been voided by the Supreme Court decision outlawing restrictive covenants, but its validity in actuality apparently still stands.

Deauville Gardens is certainly not a rich man's housing development. Most of the residents are working people. Many of them are foreign-born and have had little opportunity for education.

Now that I have given a little descriptive background, I will come to the direct quotes—the ones which appeared to me most significant in the two community opinion polls.

Local Residents Speak

A middle-aged housewife: "There's no discrimination in the community: I don't care if he moves in."

An older housewife with a German accent: "People are human: it don't matter what color they are."

A middle-aged man: "The time is not ripe yet."

A middle-aged housewife: "Why does he want to come here? There are plenty of fine colored homes in North Amityville."

A middle-aged man: "I don't discriminate, but I wouldn't want one as a neighbor."

A young wife: "My father and mother (living in the same house) think differently, but we (she and her husband) think the community should be willing to stick it out with Wilson if Wilson is willing to stick it out with us."

A young wife: "I'm against it: they just don't live the same as we do. I've lived with the high ones and the low ones. You should speak to my husband."

Her husband, who said he belongs to the auxiliary police: "If the niggers move in, I'll sell out. New York and Long Island are infiltrated with them."

A middle-aged housewife: "I don't care: I'm in my house: they're in theirs."

A woman: "I'm against it. I don't want to have any muggings around here."

An old man with pronounced foreign accent: "In every nationality there's good people and there's bad people."

A middle-aged man: "I got 5 kids. You think I want my kids to become dope fiends? Before, we never had any dope out this way. Did you read about that case in the papers?

And what about the property values?"

A middle-aged housewife: "I'm not prejudiced, but I don't want them here."

A housewife who volunteered that she is Jewish: "Some say that Negroes would turn it into a slum. There are plenty of white people who would turn it into a slum."

An old Irishman: "The whole thing was just a publicity stunt for Eleanor Roosevelt." (His reference was to an NAACP meeting in Amityville at which she spoke. Actually the meeting had been planned before the fires. But the Irishman's theory was that Negroes had set the fires to give her something to talk about.)

A middle-aged housewife: "They seemed nice people, but once one family moves in, another follows."

A Divided Community

The total score on the two polls was 15 opposed to Wilson's moving in; 11 not opposed; and 5 refusing to talk. Although, as indicated by these figures, opinion varied considerably, all but 4 of the 31 persons questioned strongly condemned the setting of the fires and stated that regardless of their opinions on Negroes, that was no way to settle the issue.

Two of those who did not assail the fire-setting asserted that the fires had been accidental. The other two suggested that Negroes had set the fires to gain publicity. Almost all of those questioned resented the publicity which resulted from the fires.

Most of those opposing Wilson's moving in cited, among other reasons, their fear of a decrease in property values. The bugaboo of future interracial marriage, often raised on such occasions, was not mentioned. Mrs. Philip Hartman, wife of the head of the Civic Association, expressed the opinion that community sentiment was not hostile to Wilson.

All but two of those questioned in the two polls answered questions calmly, without exhibiting the hysterical hostility which marked the Cicero situation in 1951 [in Cicero, IL, there were race riots over housing conditions].

There was no indication that members of the community would have instituted mob action against Wilson if he had moved in.

In the two polls all those who commented on Wilson personally—including the persons who were opposed to his moving in—did so favorably. Had Wilson occupied his house, he undoubtedly would have been accepted in the community within a matter of months—although the first few months would have been disagreeable, particularly for the kids.

In November 1950 the Nelson's, a Negro couple, moved into Gano, a small southern Ohio village despite threats from the residents and within a year they were accepted by the community. This story I told in detail in the December 1951 issue of *The Crisis*.

Peaceful Integration

There are countless instances of Negroes moving into white communities and becoming peacefully integrated, but these cases are never publicized. One recent instance about which I happen to know first hand is that of Dr. Arthur Falls, Negro surgeon, and his wife. A few months ago they moved into their home in Western Springs, a Chicago suburb which until that time had been lily-white, they have been living there peacefully ever since. They occupied the house only after an 18-month legal battle in which the Western Springs Park District had sought to condemn their property on the pretext that it was to be made into a park. The only situations which make newspaper headlines, however, are those like in Cicero and Amityville.

To come back to Wilson, Dr. Eugene Reed of the Amityville branch of the NAACP aptly described the outcome as "a shameful victory for the forces of hate and bigotry." One encouraging fact is that as a result of the newspaper publicity Wilson has received a number of offers of possible homes in other outlying communities. So maybe next summer he will have the good fortune to secure a home where his kids will not be the victims of racial prejudice.

Integration May Not Be the Answer

James Farmer

In the following article, James Farmer discusses a difficult issue many blacks faced. According to Farmer, although the traditional rallying cry was for integration, many middle-class blacks who did successfully integrate white neighborhoods and white universities were made to feel like traitors. The deep issue, Farmer believes, is whether black Americans should assimilate into white culture, or assert themselves while preserving racial unity. In the past, he argues, the dominant answer to this question favored assimilation, and the goal was a color-blind society. As he sees it, however, efforts to achieve this goal have failed, and it is no longer the aspiration of many in the black community. Instead, Farmer says, many blacks favor a willful segregation, in which they, as he says, "preserve, cherish, and develop the ghetto, and love the black self." Moreover, according to Farmer, white liberals, who long helped the civil rights and desegregation cause, have to abandon the paternalism they have toward blacks.

As you read, consider the following questions:
1. According to Farmer, what dilemma do blacks in America face?
2. What reasons might some blacks have, according to Farmer, for resisting integration?
3. What does Farmer think the traditional role of the white liberal has been, and why does he think it ought to change?

Excerpted from "Are White Liberals Obsolete in the Black Struggle?" by James Farmer, *Progressive*, January 1968. Copyright © 1968 by the *Progressive*. Reprinted with permission.

Several months ago I received a telephone call from a stranger. The caller identified himself as a Negro and said that he was confused. He felt he was damned if he did and damned if he didn't.

"Just a few years ago," he said, "civil rights leaders were saying that the creative and radical thing to do was to break down Jim Crow by integrating white neighborhoods." So he and his bride met the challenge and battled their way into a lily white suburb. They overcame the vandalism and survived the physical threats and the isolation. They made it. "Now," he went on, "Negroes call us Uncle Toms and ex-colored folk for living out here with all these white people."

Soon the Los Angeles City School Board, after years of prodding by militant civil rights leaders, is expected to come up with plans for total desegregation of the city's schools. If these plans take shape, they will not now be hailed as a victory by the black community. The scattered applause which may greet the change will be smothered by the relentless opposition of those who demand local community control of ghetto schools instead of dispersal of their children.

The agenda of the black ghetto is changing rapidly. Last week's cliches have a hollow ring. Yesterday's answers have lost their relevance. If white America is bewildered by the swirl of shifting demands, it is not alone. There is lack of comprehension among many black folk, too.

Behind the rhetoric and posturing of today, a fundamental debate is rending the black community. The shallow newspaper headlines have done nothing to clarify the controversy, and the news accounts have oversimplified and distorted it. The issue is not militancy versus moderation. There are militants indeed and there are moderates, too, in both camps. Nor is "integration versus separation" the definitive division. Which is it—integration or separation—when a black student joins a campus Afro-American association after choosing freely to enter an integrated university? Then, is it youth against age? The young, it is true, carry the burden of the argument on one side, while many of their elders form the bulwark on the other. But chronology must not be confused with ideology.

Is the question, then, "black power"? How does one debate a slogan without a precise statement of its meaning?

The Deep Issue

There is an issue, however, and it is frighteningly real. The question stripped bare is this: What is the way for black Americans to find a meaning for their existence and to achieve dignity in the American context? Is it through assimilation? Or is it through racial cohesiveness?

This is not an unfamiliar debate on American soil. All immigrant groups have wrestled with it, and it has torn many asunder. In each case there have been voices speaking for group cohesion, for maintaining cultural identity, for a kind of sub-nationalism within this nation. There have also been voices urging dispersal, and assimilation, and pressing the smaller group to enter the larger group of their new national home. Invariably, in the first generation, internal insecurity of the group and external hostility toward it gave ascendancy to the voices favoring group cohesion. The greater the external pressure, the greater the cohesion. Immigrants and their descendants remained Irish-Americans, Italian-Americans, Polish-Americans, Jewish-Americans, with the accent on their original identity. As the external pressure was reduced, the voices of assimilation became more compelling. The ethnic hyphens faded, but they have never completely disappeared.

Divided Souls

Among black people, the ideological division has been of longer duration, because of their high visibility and the background of slavery. After emancipation the debate began, but in a low key. Many Negroes wanted then to return to Africa, and some did. But most sought somehow to make their way here—some as a separate people, and some as an assimilated group. What was the American Negro—or the Negro American? A black man who happened, through historical accident, to live in America, or an American who, by genetic accident, happened to be black? In 1903, W.E.B. Du Bois put the dilemma thus:

"One feels his two-ness—an American Negro, two souls, two thoughts, two unreconciled strivings, two warring ideals, in one dark body. . . .

"The history of the American Negro is the history of this strife—this longing to attain self-conscious manhood, to merge his double self into a better and truer self. . . . He would not Africanize America, for America has too much to teach the world and Africa. He would not bleach the Negro soul in a flood of white Americanism, for he knows that Negro blood has a message for the world. He simply wishes to make it possible for a man to be both a Negro and an American without being cursed and spit upon. . . ."

The ferocious quality of the debate in black America is of recent vintage, and was triggered by three failures—the failure of newly won legal and constitutional civil rights prerogatives to effect any meaningful change in the life situation of black people; the failure of the assault on segregation to halt the trend toward increasing segregation in housing and schools; and the failure of all efforts to have any discernible impact on racism in the nation's society. "Everything has changed, but everything remains the same," one hears constantly in the South. *De facto* segregation throughout the nation continues to rise. The income gap is still widening. Racism, like a miasma, is still breathed with the air.

The Goal of Assimilation

Throughout this century the ascendancy among the contending Negroes has been held by those who sought dispersal and assimilation. With the Supreme Court school desegregation decision of 1954 this ascendancy rode on a wave of euphoria. Two years ago, however, optimism receded to leave the bitter taste of hollow victories in the mouths of the black masses.

U.S. marshals escort James Meredith (center) into the newly integrated University of Mississippi in 1962.

What has been said to the black man throughout this century, by his leaders and by white liberals, is that he must think of himself as an individual and not as a member of a group, and that if, as an individual, he gained education and money he would first be acculturated and then assimilated into a racially integrated society. He would become, in reality, a white man with an invisible black skin in a color-blind community. Men of good will, black and white, bowed to the myth that proximity would, in itself, produce color-blindness. If assimilation were achieved, the black man would have no ethnic or racial identity; he would be an American distributed through every phase of the nation's life. The black ghetto would disappear; the Harlems would become nightmares of the past.

For many years no responsible leader would have suggested that improvement of educational or housing conditions in the ghetto could possibly serve any useful purpose. The ghettos were seen as an anachronism; to improve them would be to perpetuate the evil of segregation. Privately supported Negro colleges almost went bankrupt. A. Philip

Randolph was castigated in the late 1950s for urging formation of a "Negro American Labor Council." White students in integrated colleges complained that black students were not yet truly emancipated, for when two Negroes entered the dining hall they frequently sat together and talked with each other, rather than distributing themselves in the best integrated fashion. The cry was "segregation in reverse."

Efforts to implement this dispersion concept of integration obviously have failed, though some still argue for it—naively, I think. It no longer enjoys the widespread acceptance in the black community which it once had. Indeed, it is today under fierce attack. What the dispersion concept required of the black man was a kind of abnegation, a losing of himself as a black man to find himself as an American.

A Call for Unity

Its opponents argue for an ethnic cohesiveness, a finding of himself as a black man, as the urgent goal. They advocate group self-assertion. They foster pride in pigmentation, rather than white mimicry. Rather than disperse the ghetto and reject self, they would preserve, cherish, and develop the ghetto, and love the black self.

Some of the ethnic unity advocates are separationists and view the ghetto, which they seek to upgrade, as a separate community preferably to remain alienated from the body politic. Others see it as an ethnic community among many ethnic communities in our cities, and as a power fulcrum to propel the black man into the political and economic mainstream, thereby changing the mainstream significantly. So, there are debates within debates. The debates are creative and good. The truth, I am sure, will emerge somewhere between the extremes.

The black man must find himself as a black man before he can find himself as an American. He must now become a hyphenated American, discovering the hyphen so that he can eventually lose it. This involves accepting the stark reality that the black ghettos of our cities are not going to disappear in the foreseeable future. Nor is racism.

The Afro-American cannot skip the hyphenated phase in his development, and the losing of his hyphen will be more difficult for him, as I have suggested, because of his high visibility, because of the experience of slavery, and because of a racial mystique, deeply rooted in both white and Negro, which holds the Negro inferior. Paradoxically, the black man must, I think, strengthen his ghetto on the one hand, and continue to provide an exit on the other. He must build the economic and political power of the ghetto as he simultaneously fights for open-occupancy housing, which eventually will destroy the ghetto, but will provide the Negro with a new potency as a full American.

This is bound to be a long and agonizing process, encompassing a series of progressive and regressive steps—some dramatic, some prosaic, some violent, some passive. A thin line separates group self-pride and self-hate. To expect that all will walk that line without crossing it is naive. To ask that it not be walked because some will step over it is to ask the impossible. If the rhetoric of proponents of black consciousness is sometimes excessive, it is because they are trying to "de-program" themselves. They, too, are creatures of a national culture which has held them worthless. "Black is beautiful and it is so great to be black." If they shout too loudly, it is because they are shouting down the echoes of 400 years of contrary conditioning.

The Place of White Liberals

Those least capable of understanding what is happening in the ghetto today are, I hear, the white liberals. Their reaction is more than a matter of unrequited love. The new formulations of black unity fly in the face of their liberal dogmas and challenge every cliche they hold dear. Such a cliche is "breaking up the ghetto." Another is the "color-blindness" mystique. Still another is the shibboleth of inter-racialism, which requires, for instance, that every house party have at least one black guest.

But the white liberal is even more shattered by the redefinition of his role, or, more accurately, the rejection of his former role. Liberals have not hated us; they have loved us. It is the bigots who have hated us, and hate is its own bizarre kind of flattery; it pays its victims the high compliment of worthiness. But paternalistic love depreciates them. Hate says to a man that he is an equal; paternalism tells him he is a child. But what happens to paternalism when the child grows up?

The horror of racist programming in America, from womb to tomb, is that it has pictured the black man as an incompetent, a child—the "boy," "girl," and first-name syndrome—or at best it has viewed him as a little brother who must have his big brother as his keeper. Despite all protestations to the contrary, the historic Negro-liberal alliance, from the Abolitionists to today, has been on that basis. We blacks have been junior partners, not equals.

As a liberal friend wrote to me recently in response to my reply to his initial inquiry as to whether we had been wrong all these years he and I had fought together for integration, ". . . some of our long cherished cliches about the civil rights struggle do need updating. [But] . . . some things I continue to believe are absolute truths; among these is the fundamental truth that each man in fact be his brother's keeper, regardless of race . . ." Another cliche. And that is precisely the problem: liberals have been our custodians, guardians, handlers, *keepers,* but not our *brothers,* our eyeball-to-eyeball equals.

A middle-aged white lady, a mover in liberal causes for many years, asked me a few weeks ago why it is that now when the hand of friendship is offered to black people in the ghettos, often as not they bite it. I tried to explain that black people, especially of the lower economic strata, were hitherto silent, pliant, and largely invisible. But now they have found their voice. They are bursting with existence and are willing no longer to have their whole lives ordered by others. They insist upon making for themselves the decisions which determine their lives. They will make mistakes, but they must be their mistakes, their blunders. Free a man and he is not yet free. He must still free himself. This I viewed as a positive development toward participatory democracy. Help and cooperation, I argued, must be given on those terms, their terms, or not at all.

Ingrained Patterns

The worst result of the nation's racist programming is that even black people until now have absorbed the concept of themselves as inferior. It has stunted their growth. A child does not mature so long as he plays the role of a child. When he reaches adulthood, it is good that he leaves the household and rejects the parent if the parent does not begin to view him as an adult. Black people have now grown up in their self-image, and they have walked out of the house.

White liberalism has lost its relevance to the black struggle because it is emotionally and ideologically out of date. Some liberals have conquered their paternalism, and a few—a precious few—escaped the virus all along. But liberalism, on the whole, is weak in this respect.

To regain their relevance to the Negro struggle, white liberals must reorient their feelings and their thinking. They must get over seeing themselves as great white fathers and mothers, brokers of power and patronage for black people. They must learn that if they stoop down to offer, in the missionary way, the hand of friendship, the offer will be rejected, the hand bitten. If they offer it laterally, it will be circled warily, eyed suspiciously, then perhaps taken gingerly and tentatively.

The coming of age of the Negro has been psychological. But it is also political. The recent elections [1967] in Cleveland, Gary, Virginia, and several counties in Mississippi demonstrated that the black vote has matured in the grandest American tradition. The Negro electorate no longer is content to deprecate itself by having whites as its exclusive political custodians. It no longer is willing to be partner to the myth that political decision-making is white men's work. This shakes to its roots the urban coalition which has kept the Democratic kite aloft. The "tail" of the alliance has moved up front to join labor, liberals, ethnic blocs, and professional political machines as part of the kite itself. The Democratic Party must now accommodate to this new development or face disaster in 1968.

Control of the Ghetto

The new black maturation, apparent for some time in the psychological sense and now visible in the political arena, has encompassed the economic and educational areas only in demand, not yet in performance. Economically the ghettos are still colonies; the income-producing properties are owned by absentees, and the inhabitants are consumers paying inflated prices. A balance of payments position like theirs would cause England's Prime Minister Harold Wilson to do more than devalue the pound.

Ghetto folk are now demanding that the outward flow of dollars be reversed and that economic control of their communities be turned over to those who share their woes and dreams. None but the lunatic fringe among them clings to the bootstrap illusion that Negroes can do it all alone. Most are keenly aware that they lack the boots—the capital, the technical know-how, the managerial skills. But help from whites must be consultative and advisory; the decisions must be made by the Negroes in the ghettos. They want industries to invest in their communities, and a few are beginning to do so—to build plants, to grant franchises, to train managers. It is mandatory, though, that such properties, when built, be turned over to the local community people—when trained—to run.

In Watts, Aerojet Corporation has built a subsidiary, the Watts Manufacturing Company, which makes tents and allied products. Watts people have been trained to run the plant from top to bottom. Plans are being made to allow the five hundred employees to purchase stock in the company. The Watts Manufacturing Company, alone, will not save Watts, but it is a start toward providing ghetto dwellers with some measure of control over their economic destiny.

The demand for control over their own future is nowhere so compelling as in the educational realm. After more than a decade of using every device available in a vain attempt to get their children into white schools, in the hope that white power would insure quality education because white children were their classmates, black parents have reversed their field. The demand, as yet unachieved, is now for local community control of ghetto schools. School boards have failed to integrate and failed to educate black children, so now black parents around the country are mounting insistent campaigns for decentralization of authority, giving them control over administrators and curricula in ghetto schools. They could hardly do worse than the school boards—witness the widening gap in learning, from grades one through twelve, between ghetto youngsters and others. They might do much better, for they have one thing which the school boards have lacked: a passionate concern for their children's education and future.

The debate will rage on between cohesiveness and dispersion. Ascendancy of one camp or the other will be determined ultimately not by rhetoric, and not even by leadership, as much as by events. Events today seem to be racing to the side of the spirited new force—cohesion—and I think that is right and good for the black man at this historical juncture.

Racial Equality Is More Important than Racial Integration

New Republic

The following article, published as an editorial in the *New Republic* of December 18, 1971, discusses busing as a means of ensuring integrated schools. In the previous week's issue, the *New Republic* had argued against busing, and in the week from which this article is drawn, its editorial, perhaps in response to a flurry of letters to the editor, expands and defends the magazine's position on busing. Although it is adamantly opposed to legal segregation and supports racial equality, the magazine is less certain that racial equality requires full integration. In particular, it notes that efforts to integrate schools through busing come at the cost of breaking up communities and neighborhood schools. Furthermore, the magazine argues, many white middle-class parents resist busing by moving away, or by placing their children in private schools, which tends to damage the quality of the public schools. According to the *New Republic*, the best way to achieve racial equality may be through ensuring that all public schools, be they white or black, are good schools. This, the magazine believes, is a more important goal than desegregation itself.

As you read, consider the following questions:
1. According to the editorial, what are the problems with busing?
2. How does the editorial compare de jure segregation to de facto segregation?

3. What are the key assumptions upon which the magazine's argument rests?

Our correspondence attests to the intensity of feeling on the
subject of busing. What is the nature of the controversy?
Hard-core racist politicians to the side, very few people any
longer favor the maintenance of segregated schools, and it is
plain that in many places some busing is an indispensable device for dismantling a previously segregated school system.
The archetypical case would be one where segregation was
itself maintained by busing. But what is meant by segregated
schools, and why is it imperative that school segregation be
abolished? The kind of segregation to which the 1954
Supreme Court decision in *Brown v. Board of Education*
was addressed had been imposed by law. Such segregation
was found mainly in the South, but has existed in less pervasive fashion elsewhere, being enforced there not by formal
law, but by more or less covert official connivance. It is nonetheless offensive for that. Segregation of this sort must be up-
rooted, for moral reasons if no other. It is intolerably wrong
for governments to enforce in any fashion the separation of
the races, and thus inevitably to proclaim that one race is superior to the other. In addition, evidence gathered since the
decision in *Brown* suggests that under certain conditions the
education of black children is improved when they are
moved from a segregated school situation into one with
white children. That is the finding of the Coleman Report.

Two Important Questions
Two further questions arise, however, which are frequently
begged, though they are distinct and must be faced. One is
whether racial concentration in the schools that results
from housing patterns and other factors, is no less morally
intolerable than segregation enforced by official action.
The other is whether racial balance in schools is a necessary, or necessarily the best, means of giving black children
a better education.

The condition of racial imbalance that arises out of residential patterns and other such factors is called *de facto*. Legally enforced segregation is called *de jure*. A distinction between the two has been assumed to exist ever since *Brown v. Board of Education*, and the Supreme Court reiterated this assumption in its decision of last spring which sanctioned busing. The Court has declined all opportunities to reexamine or blur the distinction. Some lower federal courts have done so, but not the Supreme Court. Nor has the Supreme Court ever said that when one or another instance of officially induced segregation is found in northern school districts that are otherwise not segregated by law, the remedy must be the institution of racial balance, chiefly through busing in the entire school district. That is our understanding of the matter. In these northern cases the issue is thus not obedience to the Constitution as defined by the Court, but rather, what ought national policy to be, and ought it to be made by the courts or the legislature?

If it is not equally a moral imperative to abolish *de facto* racial concentration in the public schools as it is to disestablish legally enforced segregation, then rational policymakers must consider costs and benefits. The most sanguine reading of the Coleman Report and other available data does not lead us to believe that the attainment of racial balance in the schools is the only, or always the most effective, way to improve the education of black children. The demography of many areas is such that the conditions of balance in which the Coleman Report found educational improvement, are unobtainable. Moreover, racial balance can often be achieved only by sacrificing other social and educational values, chiefly a sense of community. Not universally, but often, busing aimed at assuring racial balance carries very high costs, entails not only the expenditure of funds which are in short supply and could be put to other uses, but of political and administrative resources which are also not in unlimited supply and for which other fruitful employment could be found. Finally, since the country is not prepared to pay the additional costs of closing private schools or incorporating them into the public system, or of restricting the freedom of residential choice which the upper and middle class enjoy, busing not infrequently fails to achieve its goal of racial balance, even after all its other costs have been borne.

Achieving Racial Balance

Opponents of racial imbalance are concerned, no less than we, with the short-changing of black children. But they are persuaded that only efforts to achieve racial balance, at whatever cost, will yield the desired educational returns. For our part, we would not cut off efforts in that direction: racial balance is an achievable, and for the moment, sufficient objective in many places. In many others, however, we are not so confident that it can be achieved. Nor are we sure what an "ideal" balance is in each instance. Despite the conclusions of the Coleman Report, we suspect that when a court or legislative body assumes it knows the precise, ideal, black-white ratio, experience will often upset that judgment. There are a great many districts where "balance" can be imposed only by somehow breaking up established communities or breaking up established neighborhood schools. We have seen both these things happen. But how much that breakup contributes to better education for black and white is an open question. Because it is, we would like to see far more resources and energy allocated to alternative approaches. That, we take it, is what Charles Hamilton, the black political scientist at Harvard, has in mind when he says, ". . . we should be concerned essentially with quality education, and not with the superficial bringing together of black and white students. . . . The bringing together of black and white students has been primary in our thinking as a result of the pre-1954 mentality. I think that those who do not focus on something else are failing to adapt to the times."

A Better Solution

This position is no sort of retreat from the fight against segregation in the South or North. It does rest on the proposition that conditions of racial, ethnic and class residential separation exist and are reflected in the schools, and they are not morally objectionable to the same degree as legally enforced segregation and possibly not morally objectionable at all. This position does reject as inherently implausible and inadmissibly invidious, the notion that the only way black children can be better educated is to place them next to white children. Finally the position rests on what we consider to be the realistic conclusion that unless quite radical measures are taken to restrict middle-class mobility, there are many places in the country—and they are the places where better than half the blacks live—in which for the foreseeable future the model of racial balance subsumed by the Coleman Report is beyond our reach. Something more productive than banging one's head against the stone wall of this reality should, we believe, be attempted. Neither Congress nor anyone else knows exactly how to improve the education of black children. But we ought to try to find ways.

The busing issue has been exploited cynically by people who don't give a hang whether black kids get a good education or not, and who camouflage their racism or indifference in high-blown rhetoric about neighborhood schools or "freedom of choice" or what have you. But that does not excuse others from their responsibility to distinguish when, where and how busing does or does not contribute to improving and equalizing educational opportunities. In some places it is a convenience, in some a necessity, in others an incubus.

Racial Violence in the North

Time

The following article, published in *Time* magazine in 1974, focuses on the rioting and violence that broke out in Boston in response to court-ordered busing of students. The busing, which was designed to ensure integrated classrooms despite de facto residential segregation, provoked outrage from many residents. The details of the plan involved busing students from the predominately black Roxbury neighborhood into South Boston, which was predominately white Catholic, and busing white students from South Boston into Roxbury. As the article notes, however, this time when racial violence broke out, it was not in the southern states, but in a northern city. According to *Time*, Boston's image as a progressive and enlightened place is a myth, and it quotes sources who attribute the rioting to racism and to the view that it was still possible to resist integration successfully.

As you read, consider the following questions:

1. Why does *Time* claim that to those who know Boston, the outbreak of violence should not have been surprising?
2. To what do the white residents of South Boston attribute their resistance to busing?
3. What role did the police play in the violence? How does this compare to the role they played in violence in the South?

The front-page picture showed a terrified black man cling-ing to a railing as whites clawed at his shirt. Headlines summarized the sorry situation: SCHOOL SITUATION WORS-ENS, VIOLENCE SPREADS, BLACKS URGE FEDERAL ACTION. It might have been Birmingham or Biloxi in the 1960s—but it was Boston, last week.

As the court-ordered desegregation of Boston's public schools went into its fourth week, an explosion seemed im-minent. "We can no longer maintain either the appearance or the reality of public safety," Mayor Kevin H. White said in a letter to Federal Judge W. Arthur Garrity, who had is-sued the desegregation ruling last June 21. Added White, who asked Garrity to send in federal marshals to help en-force the ruling: "Violence which once focused on the schools and buses is now engulfing the entire community in racial confrontation."

Much of the violence took place along Dorchester Street, a four-lane thoroughfare that is the main artery of South Boston, the center of opposition to forced busing. With feel-ings running high over the busing order, "Southie" swarmed with police, including 300 members of the elite Tactical Pa-trol Force brought in to disperse crowds and protect the buses bringing black students to the area's previously all-white schools. The heavy police presence increased tension among Southie's resentful Irish residents, and one evening a brick was heaved through the windshield of a cruising T.P.F. squad car. When the officers tried to arrest a suspect, two dozen Southie toughs set upon them, and the police lost the man in the crowd. The next night two dozen T.P.F. officers burst into the jampacked Rabbit Inn on Dorchester Street. As many as eight patrons were reported injured. Some Southies are convinced that the T.P.F. raid was an outright reprisal for the previous night's incident; the police claim that they were merely answering a distress call.

Warning Shots

When school resumed last week, Southie was in an even uglier mood; buses carrying black students were greeted with jeers and rocks. At one point, a Haitian immigrant named Jean-Louis André Yvon, 33, turned unwittingly onto Dorchester Street. Some 35 people surrounded Yvon's car, smashed his windshield and pulled him out. Someone shouted, "Get the nigger!" Yvon fled for the porch of a nearby house and clung to the railing as youths battered him with clubs. Only after a white policeman drew his pistol and fired some warning shots was a dazed and bleeding Yvon finally rescued. "He would have been dead if I hadn't fired," the policeman said later.

Trouble broke out the next day in predominantly black Roxbury. Black students roamed the streets, stoning cars and throwing rocks at the few white pedestrians. A white cab driver was hospitalized. Police let only black drivers into the area. "We just don't have enough men to protect you," a deputy police superintendent told white reporters. "Don't look left or right. Just keep driving until you get to the suburbs."

The violence was dismaying, but to those who know Boston, it should not have been surprising. The city's image as the Athens of America is a rosy distortion. Boston's renowned academic and cultural institutions seldom touch the lives of most of its 624,900 residents, who are mainly lower-middle class in income and outlook, fiercely loyal to their own ethnic backgrounds and neighborhoods. "Boston is a racist city and always has been," says Boston College Law Professor Leonard Strickman.

Lay Waste

For residents of Southie, a physically and psychologically isolated "town," Garrity's integration ruling was like an order to lay their community to waste. As one anguished Southie mother put it last week, "If they can tell you where to send your kids to school, they can tell you where to work, they can tell you anything, they can take anything away from you."

The basic intent of Garrity's ruling was to improve the racial balance of the 80 city schools (out of 200) that were more than 50% black. This was also the intent of the state's Elimination of Racial Imbalance Law. Passed in 1965 but blocked through nine years of litigation and defiance by the largely Irish Catholic Boston school committee, the law was finally repealed this spring, but by then the issue was in the hands of the federal court. Judge Garrity ordered desegregation to begin under a plan drawn up by the state board of education.

About 45,000 of Boston's 94,000 pupils have now been assigned to schools they would not normally have attended. This involves busing more than 18,000 students, including 8,510 whites. Under the plan, the South Boston and Roxbury school districts have been combined; 1,271 white pupils from South Boston have been assigned to Roxbury or other neighborhoods and 1,746 nonwhites have been assigned to Southie's schools.

When school started this fall, Southie swiftly developed what some residents call a "Belfast mentality," the attitude of a beleaguered and persecuted minority. Southie parents argue that forced busing not only will destroy the concept of community schools but also compel their own children to travel into high-crime neighborhoods. Many Southie Irish Catholics feel betrayed by their own leaders: Humberto Cardinal Medeiros, who has given strong moral support to the busing plan and refuses to let parents enroll their children in parochial schools just to avoid it; Senator Edward Kennedy, whose probusing stand made him a target for curses and raw eggs at a recent antibusing rally; and Mayor White, who is often referred to in Southie as Mayor Black.

Southie was heartened by President Ford's statement at his press conference last week that "the court decision . . . was not the best solution to quality education in Boston . . . I respectfully disagree with the judge's order." But elsewhere in Boston, the remark was widely attacked as insensitive and irresponsible. The mayor accused the President of trying to "taunt this city into becoming another Little Rock."

Harvard Social Psychologist Thomas Pettigrew believes Southie turned to violence partly because it still believes integration can be prevented. "When a community senses that change is going to take place come hell or high water," he says, "you don't get the violence. In Boston more than in Little Rock, you have had people who have been told for years that busing is not inevitable, that it will not happen here." Last week most Southie parents were still keeping their children out of public schools.

High Tensions

Despite White's plea for marshals, none were ordered into Boston, and the mayor's critics suspected that pure politics was behind his appeal to Garrity. White backed his request with the claim that city resources had been strained to the breaking point. A police force with only 2,000 active officers cannot indefinitely station one-half of them in just one area of the city. But why not ask for state police or National Guardsmen rather than federal marshals? Possibly because the state lawmen could only be mobilized by Republican Governor Francis Sargent, one of Democrat White's chief rivals.

Though Garrity denied the mayor's request, he did accede to a black demand for additional protection. By the time 300 riot-helmeted state troopers and 125 other state lawmen moved into Southie to relieve the overworked T.P.F., however, the violence seemed to be subsiding. "It must be hard guarding against all us women with shopping bags," a gray-haired housewife needled a trooper outside South Boston High.

At week's end, as the first full month of busing ended, Boston could count itself lucky that so far no lives had been lost. But tensions remained high as still another Northern city wrestled with a problem that was once regarded as peculiarly Southern.

CHRONOLOGY

1865
The Thirteenth Amendment makes slavery illegal.

1868
The Fourteenth Amendment extends citizenship to blacks and guarantees due process and equal protection under the law to all citizens.

1870
The Fifteenth Amendment extends the right to vote to black men.

1875
Congress passes a civil rights act guaranteeing equal rights to blacks in public accommodations and jury duty.

1881
Tennessee segregates railroad cars. It is followed by Florida (1887); Mississippi (1888); Texas (1889); Louisiana (1890); Alabama, Kentucky, Arkansas, and Georgia (1891); South Carolina (1898); North Carolina (1899); Virginia (1900); Maryland (1904); and Oklahoma (1907).

1883
The Supreme Court rules that the Civil Rights Act of 1875 is unconstitutional.

1895
Booker T. Washington, a prominent black leader, urges a policy of gradualism and says that blacks and whites can live separately yet prosper together.

1896

In *Plessy v. Ferguson*, the Supreme Court rules that "separate but equal" facilities do not violate the Fourteenth Amendment, and thus gives legal sanction to Jim Crow segregation laws.

1909

The National Association for the Advancement of Colored People (NAACP) is founded.

1910

The Baltimore City Council approves an ordinance designating the boundaries of black and white neighborhoods. Similar ordinances follow in other cities in the South.

1913

The federal government begins to segregate its workplaces, rest rooms, and lunchrooms.

1918

Blacks begin migrating north in huge numbers. Between 1910 and 1930, the black population in the South drops by about 1 million while the black population in the North grows by about 1 million.

1936

Jesse Owens wins four gold medals at the Olympics, which take place in Nazi Germany. He later says, "I wasn't invited to shake hands with Hitler, but I wasn't invited to the White House to shake hands with the president either."

1941

President Franklin D. Roosevelt issues an executive order ending discrimination in defense industries.

1944

Swedish sociologist Gunnar Myrdal publishes *An American Dilemma,* a landmark exploration of race relations in the United States.

1945

Ebony, a new magazine for blacks, hits newsstands and promptly sells out.

1946

President Harry S. Truman creates the President's Committee on Civil Rights.

1947

Jackie Robinson becomes the first black player in Major League Baseball.

1948

The Supreme Court rules in *Shelley v. Kraemer* that blacks can live in all-white neighborhoods. President Truman orders desegregation of the armed forces.

1950

The Supreme Court rules in *Sweatt v. Painter* that the University of Texas cannot bar blacks from its law school.

1954

In *Brown v. Board of Education of Topeka, Kansas,* the Supreme Court rules that the "separate but equal" doctrine has no place in education.

1955

In May, the Supreme Court orders southern states to implement desegregation with "all deliberate speed." In December, Rosa Parks refuses to change seats on a bus in Montgomery, Alabama, and her arrest leads to a boycott of the bus system. It lasts over a year, until the Supreme Court outlaws bus segregation in the city.

1956

In January, Autherine Lucy is admitted to the University of Alabama following a Supreme Court order. Lucy is later expelled after white students riot. In March, one hundred congressmen from the South sign the Southern Manifesto, which urges resistance to federal desegregation orders.

1957

In January, the Southern Christian Leadership Conference is founded, with Martin Luther King Jr. as president. In August, the Voting Rights Bill, the first major civil rights legislation in more than seventy-five years, is passed by Congress. In September, on what was to be Little Rock Central High's first day as a desegregated school, Arkansas National Guardsmen under orders of Governor Orval Faubus prevent nine black students from entering. Eventually, after President Eisenhower orders one thousand paratroopers and ten thousand National Guardsmen to Little Rock, the school is desegregated.

1958

In September, three all-white schools in Virginia, Warren County High School, Lane High School, and Venerable Elementary School, choose to close rather than integrate.

1959

In January, the Virginia Supreme Court of Appeals rules in *Harrison v. Day* that the school closings violate the state constitution, which requires Virginia to "maintain an efficient system of public free schools throughout the State." In February, twenty-one black students integrate previously all-white schools in Norfolk and Arlington, Virginia.

1960

In February, sit-ins in Greensboro, North Carolina, initiate a wave of similar protests through southern states. In April, the Student Nonviolent Coordinating Committee is founded in Raleigh, North Carolina. In May, President Eisenhower signs the Civil Rights Act of 1960, which authorizes the appointment of federal referees to oversee black voter registration in southern counties. In December, the Supreme Court's ruling in *Boynton v. Virginia* outlaws segregation in interstate bus and railroad facilities.

1961

At many bus stops in the South, violent whites await the Freedom Riders, who are trying to end discrimination in the interstate bus system.

1962

Under orders from President John F. Kennedy, federal marshals escort to campus James Meredith, the first black student to enroll at the University of Mississippi. Two students are killed when a riot breaks out.

1963

Martin Luther King Jr. and others are arrested during an April march in Birmingham, Alabama, one of the most severely segregated cities in the country. In June, Governor George C. Wallace stands in the doorway of a University of Alabama building to signal his blocking of the admission of two black students; President Kennedy orders the Alabama National Guard to clear the way. That same month, Medgar Evers, an NAACP field secretary, is murdered in his driveway in Jackson, Mississippi. In August, King delivers his famous "I Have a Dream" speech at the March on Washington, the largest civil rights demonstration in U.S. history. In September, four young black girls are killed when the Sixteenth Street Baptist Church in Birmingham, Alabama, is firebombed.

1964

In June, James Chaney, a young black activist, and Andrew Goodman and Michael Schwerner, two white activists, are murdered in Mississippi. In July, President Lyndon B. Johnson signs the Civil Rights Act of 1964, which bars discrimination in public accommodations and in hiring. In December, King accepts the Nobel Peace Prize.

1965

In March, during a march from Selma, Alabama, to Montgomery, state troopers attack the crowd with tear gas and batons. In November, the Supreme Court rules against the Freedom of Choice plan in Richmond, Virginia, on the grounds that teachers are still segregated.

1968

In March, the Kerner Commission warns that America is becoming "two societies, one black, one white, separate and unequal." In April, Martin Luther King Jr. is assassinated in Memphis, Tennessee. Riots break out in every major city in the country except Indianapolis. President Johnson signs the Civil Rights Act of 1968, which contains a clause barring discrimination against blacks in the sale or rental of most housing.

1969

In October, the Supreme Court rules in *Alexander v. Holmes* that southern school districts are to desegregate "at once."

1971

In April, the Supreme Court rules in *Swann v. Charlotte-Mecklenburg Board of Education* that busing is a legitimate means to achieve public school integration. Court-ordered busing plans in cities such as Charlotte, Boston, and Denver are largely unpopular, and often violently opposed. They continue, however, until the late 1990s.

1973

In May, Thomas Bradley is elected the first black mayor of Los Angeles. In October, Maynard H. Jackson is elected the first black mayor of Atlanta.

1974

In June, a U.S. district court judge rules that the Boston School Committee knowingly segregated schoolchildren and denied quality education to children because of their race.

1978

Seattle becomes the largest city in the country to desegregate its schools without a court order. As part of the "Seattle Plan," nearly one-quarter of the city's students are bused.

1983

In June, the last racial classification law in the United States—a stipulation that defined the criterion for being black as having $\frac{1}{32}$ Negro blood—is repealed by Louisiana's state legislature.

FOR FURTHER RESEARCH

Books

Ralph David Abernathy, *And the Walls Came Tumbling Down*. New York: Harper & Row, 1989.

Daisy Bates, *The Long Shadow of Little Rock*. New York: David McKay, 1962.

Albert P. Blaustein and Clarence Clyde Fergeson Jr., *Desegregation and the Law: The Meaning and Effect of the School Segregation Cases*. New Brunswick, NJ: Rutgers University Press, 1957.

Albert P. Blaustein and Robert L. Zangrando, eds., *Civil Rights and the American Negro: A Documentary History*. New York: Washington Square Press, 1968.

Taylor Branch, *Parting the Waters: America in the King Years, 1954–1963*. New York: Simon and Schuster, 1988.

Vicki L. Crawford, Jacqueline Anne Rouse, and Barbara Woods, eds., *Women in the Civil Rights Movement*. Brooklyn, NY: Carlson Publishing, 1990.

Ralph Ellison, *Invisible Man*. New York: Vintage Books, 1995.

James Farmer, *Lay Bare the Heart: An Autobiography of the Civil Rights Movement*. New York: Arbor House, 1985.

Ronald P. Formisano, *Boston Against Busing: Race, Class, and Ethnicity in the 1960s and 1970s*. Chapel Hill: University of North Carolina Press, 1991.

Henry Hampton, Steve Fager, and Sarah Flynn, *Voices of Freedom: An Oral History of the Civil Rights Movement from the 1950s Through the 1980s*. New York: Bantam Books, 1990.

Langston Hughes, *The Fight for Freedom: The Story of the NAACP*. New York: W.W. Norton, 1962.

Martin Luther King Jr., *I Have a Dream: Writings and Speeches That Changed the World*. Ed. J. Melvin. San Francisco: Harper, 1986.

Richard Kluger, *Simple Justice: The History of* Brown v. Board of Education *and Black America's Struggle for Equality*. New York: Alfred A. Knopf, 1976.

Jonathan Kozol, *Death at an Early Age: The Destruction of the Hearts and Minds of Negro Children in the Boston Public Schools*. New York: Houghton Mifflin, 1967.

J. Anthony Lukas, *Common Ground: A Turbulent Decade in the Lives of Three American Families*. New York: Vintage Books, 1985.

Arval A. Morris, *The Constitution and American Public Education*. Durham, NC: Carolina Academic Press, 1989.

Gunnar Myrdal, *An American Dilemma: The Negro Problem and Modern Democracy*. New York: Harper & Brothers, 1944.

J.W. Peltason, *Fifty-Eight Lonely Men: Southern Federal Judges and School Desegregation*. New York: Harcourt, Brace & World, 1961.

J. Harvie Wilkinson III, *From* Brown *to* Bakke: *The Supreme Court and School Integration: 1954–1978*. New York: Oxford University Press, 1979.

Benjamin Munn Ziegler, ed., *Desegregation and the Supreme Court: Problems in American Civilization*. Boston: D.C. Heath, 1958.

Periodicals

Linda Charlton, "Maryland County Begins School Desegregation Plan," *New York Times,* January 30, 1973.

Ellis Cose, "What's White, Anyway?" *Newsweek*, September 18, 2000.

Jerome Cramer, "Judging Where the Bus Can Stop: The Supreme Court Finds a 'Good Faith' Limit for Desegregation," *Time*, January 28, 1991.

Paul Delaney, "N.A.A.C.P. to Press Schools in North: Seeks Full Desegregation Within Five Years," *New York Times*, November 28, 1974.

B. Drummond, "Civil Rights Optimism Rekindled; Ruling for Louisville Busing Gives New Hope to Advocates," *New York Times*, December 25, 1974.

Ted Gest, "A Case That Shook the U.S. Is Back," *U.S. News & World Report*, December 1, 1986.

———, "School Desegregation Grinds to a Halt in South," *U.S. News & World Report*, May 21, 1984.

Robin D.G. Kelly, "Integration: What's Left?" *Nation*, December 14, 1998.

John Kifner, "Four Boston High Schools Hit by Walkouts," *New York Times*, December 13, 1974.

———, "Judge in Boston Defied on Busing," *New York Times*, December 17, 1974.

John Leland and Vern E. Smith, "Echoes of Little Rock," *Newsweek*, September 29, 1997.

John Lewis, "Forgiving George Wallace," *New York Times*, September 16, 1998.

Ed Magnuson, "A House Divided: Yonkers, N.Y. Becomes a Symbol of White Resistance to Integration," *Time*, August 15, 1988.

Agnes E. Meyer, "Race and the Schools," *Atlantic*, January 1958.

Eliza Paschall, "A Southern Point of View," *Atlantic*, May 1960.

Adolph Reed, "Looking Back at *Brown*," *Progressive*, June 1994.

Robert Reinhold, "To Some Blacks, the Bus Ride Isn't Worth It," *New York Times*, July 14, 1974.

Michael Riley, "Confessions of a Former Segregationist," *Time*, March 2, 1992.

William Safire, "South Boston High," *New York Times*, November 11, 1974.

Jack E. White, "Why We Need to Raise Hell," *Time*, April 29, 1996.

David Whitman and Dorian Friedman, "Busing's Unheralded Legacy," *U.S. News & World Report*, April 13, 1992.

INDEX

Acheson, Dean, 40–41
Aerojet Corporation, 177
affirmative action, 28
African Americans. *See* blacks
Albany, Georgia, 90, 91, 92–95, 96–97
Amityville, New York, 164–66
Anderson, Marian, 21
Anniston, Alabama, 122
applied religion. *See* nonviolent resistance
Arkansas. *See* Little Rock Central High School
Arkansas Gazette (newspaper), 81
armed forces
desegregation of, 22, 35
moral effect of segregation on, 35
during World War II, 21, 22
assimilation
by blacks, 161, 168, 171, 172
by immigrants, 170

baseball, 22
Belfast mentality, 187
beloved community, 121–22
Birmingham, Alabama
bombings in, 145
Freedom Rides in, 25, 122
Black, Hugo, 64
black codes, 13–15
Black Power, 161
blacks
activists, 20–21
assimilation of, 161, 168, 171, 172
association with whites is not goal of, 48
development as Americans of, 173
educational achievement of, 102, 180
employment of, 102, 105

FBI violates rights of, 87, 95–96
income gap of, 171
as junior partners in civil rights movement, 174–75
leadership class of
decline of, 127
described, 20–21
ignored basic problems, 132
importance of religion to, 109
is myth, 130–31
protests and, 127, 128, 129
strategy of, 129
life expectancy of, 102
maturity as community and nonviolent resistance, 110
migration to North of, 18, 160
must seize citizenship, 112
social system in South respects, 79
whites and
nonviolent resistance will mitigate fear of, 116
relationship in South, 54, 55–58
bombings, 145
Boston, Massachusetts, 28–29, 161, 184, 185–88
Boynton v. Virginia, 25
Brennan, William J., 64
Brotherhood of Sleeping Car Porters, 21
Brown v. Board of Education of Topeka, Kansas
background of, 22–23, 63
compliance ruling in, 23
decision in, 23, 44, 63
unanimity of, 61, 63
is abuse of power by Supreme Court, 71, 72–73
justices in, 63–64
legal objections to, 64–65, 70
violated states' rights, 68, 73

Buchanan v. Warley, 21
Burton, Harold H., 64
Bush, George H.W., 30
busing
  in Boston, 28–29, 161, 184,
    185–88
  cost of, 181
  described, 161
  goal of, 186–87
  inevitability of, 188
  negative effects of, 161–62, 179,
    182
  Nixon and, 29
  philosophy of, 28
  racial balance is not achieved by,
    182, 183
  Supreme Court and, 28, 30
  violence and, 161, 184, 185–88
    opposition to, 186, 187

Campbell, Cull, 97
Carpenter, Bill, 137
Chambers, Lenoir, 33, 61
Christianity
  brotherhood in, 50
  burning of churches, 98
  civil rights movement and, 26,
    109, 119, 120–21, 125, 134
  federal government wishes to
    replace, 78
  importance of, in South, 153
  insists on moral action, 113
  segregation is act against, 45
citizenship
  blacks must seize, 112
  Fourteenth Amendment and, 15
  privileges of, 101
Civil Rights Act (1964), 26–27,
  145
civil rights movement
  assassinations and, 29
  background of, 32, 66
  federal government is not
    advocate of, 90
  goals of, 12
  John F. Kennedy was not
    dependable ally of, 90, 91–92,
    98

leaders of
  decline of established
    organizations as, 127
  students became, 127, 128–29
  see also Congress of Racial
    Equality; National
    Association for the
    Advancement of Colored
    People
in North
  white support for, 160
  see also busing
  paternalism in, 174–75
  peak of, 32
  religion and, 26, 109, 119,
    120–21, 125, 134
  see also nonviolent resistance;
    protests
Clark, Kenneth, 117
Clark, Tom C., 64
class segregation, 19
Coleman Report, 180, 181
Coles, Robert, 150
color-blind society, 168, 172
Congress of Racial Equality
  (CORE)
  Freedom Rides and, 25, 122
  sit-ins and, 136
  during World War II, 21–22
Constitution
  First Amendment, 93, 98
  Fourteenth Amendment
    *Brown v. Board of Education
      of Topeka, Kansas* and, 23
    citizenship and, 15
    intent of, 70
    lack of enforcement legislation
      for, 98
    Lum v. Rice and, 72
    narrow interpretation of, 26
    Plessy v. Ferguson and, 16, 72
    ratification of, 64, 65
    education at time of, 71–72
  Fifteenth Amendment, 15
Cooper, Barbara, 139
crime, 39
Crisis, The (newsletter), 167

Daughters of the American Revolution, 21
Davies, Ronald N., 82
Deacons, 149
Deauville Gardens, 164–66
Declaration of Constitutional Principles, 71, 72–73
Declaration of Independence, 50
de facto segregation
  described, 12, 18–19, 160, 161, 163
  effect of de jure segregation on, 18
  of housing, 166
  increase in, 171
  is matter of national policy, 181
  poverty and, 27
  Supreme Court and, 181
de jure segregation
  Civil Rights Act and, 27
  described, 12, 160, 163
  effect on de facto segregation of, 18
  of housing, 17, 21
direct action. See nonviolent resistance
Dirksen, Everett, 26
disease, 39
Douglas, William O., 64
Du Bois, W.E.B., 20, 171

economy
  effect of desegregation on, 157
  effect of protests on, 128, 154
  in ghettos, 176–77
  nonviolent resistance and, 95
  segregation harms, 34, 37–39, 47
education
  absence of, in Constitution, 71
  achievement of blacks and, 102, 180
  desegregation of
    academic achievement and, 29
    is too slow, 104–105
    must be planned, 49
    pace of, 24, 86
    in Washington, D.C., 23
    see also Brown v. Board of

Education of Topeka, Kansas; busing; Little Rock Central High School
    equality was never attempted, 49–50
    Fourteenth Amendment and, 71–72
  higher, 24
  during Reconstruction, 16
  Supreme Court and, 21, 22
  housing and, 180
  local control of, 19, 68–69, 169, 177
  parental rights in, 72
  quality of, is more important than busing, 182
  separate but equal in, 22, 72
Eisenhower, Dwight D., 84
  desegregation of schools in Washington, D.C., by, 23
  Little Rock and, 24, 69
Elimination of Racial Imbalance Law, 187
employment
  black codes and, 14–15
  black rate of, 102, 105
  federal jobs, 22
  income gap in, 171
  is harmed by segregation, 37–38
  migration of blacks to North and, 18
ethnic unity, 172–74

Fair Employment Practices Commission, 22
Falls, Arthur, 167
Farmer, James, 161, 168
Faubus, Orval, 23–24, 69, 81–83, 84
Federal Bureau of Investigation (FBI)
  favors whites, 90, 96
  violates rights of blacks, 87, 95–96
federal government
  employment in, 22
  enforcement of court decisions by, 82, 84, 85, 87–88

Interstate Commerce
Commission, 93
is not advocate of civil rights
movement, 90
law enforcement by, is variable,
90, 92
Federal Bureau of Investigation
and, 87, 90, 95–96
segregation of facilities of,
17–18
threat of increased power of,
77–78
voter registration drives and,
142–43
during World War II, 21
see also Supreme Court
fires, 39
Ford, Gerald, 187
foreign affairs
international independence
movements and, 66
Little Rock Central High School
and, 88–89
Oxford and, 91
segregation harms, 34, 40–43,
44, 50, 51–52, 103
U.S. commitment to freedom
internationally and, 101
Frankfurter, Felix, 64
Franklin, John Hope, 59
freedom of exhaustion, 112–13
Freedom Rides
constitutionality of, 125–26
described, 25, 119, 122
goals of, 123
violence and, 122, 124, 125
Freedom to the Free (United
States Commission on Civil
Rights), 19–20

Gaines v. Canada, 21
Gandhi, Mohandas, 108, 118
Garrity, W. Arthur, 185, 187, 188
George, Walter F., 70
ghettos
disappearance of, 172
economic development of,
176–77

ethnic unity and, 173
segregation creates, 39
gradualism, 20, 110
Greensboro, North Carolina, 25
group cohesion, 170

Hall, Bobby, 96
Hamilton, Charles, 182
Harlan, John Marshall, 16–17, 64
Hartman, Mrs. Philip, 166
Henry, Patrick, 80
Herald Tribune (newspaper), 57
Hollins v. Oklahoma, 21
Hood, James, 100
Horace Mann High School, 81
housing
peaceful desegregation of, 167
restrictive covenants and, 164
segregation of
de facto, 166
de jure, 17, 21
education and, 180
growth of, 17
is less in South than in North,
57
transportation and, 13, 18–19
Supreme Court and, 21, 164
Houston, Charles, 21
Howard, Jan, 141

Ickes, Harold L., 21
Illinois, 167
immigrants, 170
interstate commerce, 26, 93

Jackson, Robert H., 64
Jefferson, Thomas, 80
Jim Crow laws
described, 16
enactment of, 32
may have had rational basis
when instituted, 58
Johnson, Lyndon B., 27
jury duty, 21

Kennedy, Edward, 187
Kennedy, John F., 100
Albany and, 90, 92–93

University of Alabama and, 69
University of Mississippi and, 24, 90, 91
was not dependable ally of civil rights movement, 90, 91–92, 98
Kennedy, Robert, 29
Keyes v. Denver, 28
Kilpatrick, James Jackson, 33, 53
King, C.B., 97
King, Martin Luther, Jr., 111
  assassination of, 29
  Federal Bureau of Investigation and, 96
  Freedom Rides and, 125
  imprisonment of, 97–98
  March on Washington and, 108
  Montgomery bus boycott and, 24
  Selma protests and, 143–44
  strategy of, 136
    nonviolent resistance and, 26
    value of retaliatory violence and, 145, 146
King, Mrs. Slater, 96
Ku Klux Klan, 25
Ku Klux Klan Act, 15

law-and-order principle, 90, 92
Lawson, James, Jr., 128
Lewis, John, 124
Little Rock Central High School
  desegregation plan for, 86–87
  effect of, on foreign affairs, 88–89
  events at, 23–24
  Faubus and, 69, 81–83, 84
Little Rock of the North, the. *See* Boston, Massachusetts
Lomax, Louis E., 127
London, Scott, 150
Los Angeles, California, 169
Lum v. Rice, 72

Madison, James, 80
Malcolm X, 29
Malone, Vivian, 100
March on Washington, 108
Marshall, Thurgood, 21

Mason, George, 80
Mays, Benjamin E., 33, 44
McCrory's, 136, 139
McLaurin v. Oklahoma State Regents, 22
Medeiros, Humberto Cardinal, 187
Meredith, James, 24, 90
Minton, Sherman, 64
Mississippi
  black codes in, 13
  Summer Project, 142–43
Montagu, Ashley, 59
Montgomery, Alabama
  bus boycott in, 24
  Freedom Rides in, 25, 124–25
Myrdal, Gunnar, 39–40, 64

Nash, Diane, 119
Nashville, Tennessee, 120
National Association for the Advancement of Colored People (NAACP)
  leadership of civil rights movement and, 130
  protests and, 128
  strategy of, 20–21, 109
National Guard
  at Little Rock Central High School, 23–24, 69, 81, 84
  at University of Alabama, 24, 69, 100, 101
  at University of Mississippi, 24
Negroes. *See* blacks
New Republic (magazine), 179
New York City, 164–66
New York Times (newspaper), 97
Nixon, Richard, 29, 30
Nobel Peace Prize, 111
nonviolent resistance
  commitment to, is not secure, 147
  costs of, 95, 117
  described, 108
  effectiveness of, 26
  elements of successful movement, 115–16
  examples of, 95

goals of, 108, 117, 120, 121–22
importance of, in civil rights
  movement, 111
maturity of blacks as
  community and, 110
moral superiority of, 111, 146
philosophy of, 25–26, 108–109,
  114–15, 116–17
religious aspects of, 119,
  120–21, 134
retaliatory violence is strategy
  of, 109, 141, 142–45, 148–49
see also sit-ins
North
de facto segregation in, 18–19
does not understand social
  system in South, 55, 57
housing is more segregated than
  in South, 57
migration of blacks to, 18, 160
racism in
  subtlety of, 165–66
  violence and, 164
  see also busing
separate but equal in, 72
white support for civil rights
  movement in, 160

Oxford, Mississippi, 90, 91

Parks, Rosa, 24
Peck, James, 122, 163
Pettigrew, Thomas, 187–88
Phillips, Ulrich Bonnell, 63
Plessy v. Ferguson
decision in, 44, 72
did not result in equality, 49–50
dissent in, 16–17
Fourteenth Amendment and, 16,
  72
higher education and, 22
police
arrest of peaceful demonstrators
  by, 135
in Albany, 90, 91, 92, 93–95
refusal to be provoked by
  demonstrators in Selma,
  144–45

sit-ins and, 137–38, 139–40
violence against, 185
violence by
  in Albany, 96–97
  in Birmingham, 25
  Supreme Court and, 96
  in Tallahassee, 140
  use of dogs, 145
poverty, 27–28, 38
President's Committee on Civil
  Rights, 22, 32–33, 34
segregation harms economy,
  37–39
segregation harms foreign
  affairs, 40–43
segregation has high social costs,
  39–40
segregation is morally wrong,
  35–37
Pritchett, Laurie, 93, 95, 97
protests
effect of, on economy, 128, 154
forms of, 94–95, 108
  bus boycotts, 24
  Freedom Rides, 119, 122–26
  marches, 25
  see also sit-ins
violence in North by
  participants, 141
were grassroots movement, 127,
  129
public facilities
inferiority of, for blacks, 12
nonviolent protests at, 95
Plessy v. Ferguson and, 16
segregation of
  growth of, 17–18
  results in wasteful duplication
    of, 38
  see also transportation

Quarterman, Ola Mae, 94

racial justice
costs of, 117
desegregation will not achieve,
  132
dignity is core of, 121, 129

is not a racial issue, 115
is religious issue, 119, 120–21
violence cannot achieve, 113–14
Randolph, Asa Philip, 21, 172
Randolph, Peyton, 79–80
Reagan, Ronald, 30
Reconstruction, 15–17
redeemed community, 121–22
Reed, Eugene, 167
Reed, Stanley F., 64
Rehnquist, William, 30
religion
  applied. See nonviolent
    resistance
  brotherhood in, 50
  burning of churches, 98
  civil rights movement and, 26,
    109, 119, 120–21, 125, 134
  federal government wishes to
    replace, 78
  importance of, in South, 153
  insists on moral action, 113
  segregation is act against, 45
restrictive covenants, 164
Roberts v. City of Boston, 72
Robinson, Jackie, 22
Roosevelt, Eleanor, 21
Roxbury (Boston, Massachusetts),
  184, 186, 187

Sears, 136
segregation
  creates ghettos, 39
  described, 12
  development of, 13
  goals of, 46–47
  growth of, 17–18
  is issue of states' rights, 75
  is morally wrong, 33, 34,
    35–37, 45–46, 47, 48, 49, 50,
    102, 103, 180
  con, 33, 54
  mandating of, 16
  results of, 12
    in education. See education
    harms economy, 34, 37–39, 47
    harms foreign affairs, 34,
      40–43, 44, 50, 51–52, 103

in housing. See housing
  is psychologically harmful, 39,
    44, 47, 48, 112–13, 121,
    174, 175
  violence against dominant
    group, 39–40
  voluntary, 161, 168
  was established by founding
    fathers, 79
  white supremacy and, 12
  see also de facto segregation; de
    jure segregation
Selma, Alabama, 25, 143–45
separate-but-equal doctrine
  education and, 22, 72
  equality was never achieved,
    49–50
  establishment of, 16–17
  results in wasteful duplication of
    facilities, 38
  Roberts v. City of Boston and,
    72
Separate Car Act, 16
sit-ins
  described, 25, 135, 137
  economic effect of, 128
  importance of, 133–34
  police and, 137–38, 139–40
  public support for desegregation
    and, 135
  spontaneity of, 128
  strategy of, 136
  trials of participants in, 138–39
  violence and, 134, 139, 140
Sitton, Claude, 97
slavery, legacy of, 13, 27–28, 32,
  102–103
Smith, Kelly Miller, 128
South
  black codes in, 13–15
  has been wronged, 54
  housing is less segregated than
    in North, 57
  importance of religion in, 153
  Jim Crow laws in, 16, 32, 58
  limitations on suffrage in, 35–36
  during Reconstruction, 15–17
  social system in

described, 32
individuals as passive members
of, 152, 155–58
is being destroyed, 73
is dual society, 54, 55–58
respects blacks, 79
was home to many founding
fathers, 79–80
white supremacy in
described, 33
is unifying principle of, 61, 63,
76
segregation and, 12
truth of, 53, 59–60
South Boston, Massachusetts,
184, 185–88
South Carolina, 13–15
Southern Manifest, 71, 72–73
Southern Regional Council, 91
sports, 22
states' rights
Brown v. Board of Education of
Topeka, Kansas violated, 68,
73
segregation is issue of, 75
was established by founding
fathers, 78
Stephens, Patricia, 135
Stephens, Priscilla, 136, 137–38
Stewart, Potter, 64
Strickman, Leonard, 186
suburbs, 19
suffrage
Constitution and, 15
election of blacks to office and,
176
legislation to protect, 98
limitations in South on, 35–36
during Reconstruction, 15–16
voter registration drives and, 25,
142–43
Supreme Court
abuse of power by, 71, 72–73
appointees to, 29, 30
authority of, 86
busing and, 28, 30
de facto segregation and, 181
housing and, 21, 164

injunctions to protect
constitutional rights and, 98
violence by police and, 96
see also individual Court cases
Swann v. Charlotte-Mecklenburg,
28
Sweatt v. Painter, 22
Swig, Jim, 124

Tallahassee, Florida, 140
taxes, 39
Time (magazine), 184
Title VII, 27
To Secure These Rights
(President's Committee on Civil
Rights), 22, 32–33, 34
transportation
housing segregation and, 13,
18–19
interstate commerce regulation
and, 26, 93
segregation of
growth of, 17
Jim Crow laws and, 58
Plessy v. Ferguson and, 16
protests against, 24, 94–95
Freedom Rides, 25, 119,
122–26
Montgomery bus boycott, 24
results in wasteful duplication
of facilities, 38
Supreme Court and, 24–25
Truman, Harry S., 22, 32–33, 34

Uncle Toms, 169
United States Commission on
Civil Rights, 19–20
Universal Negro Improvement
Organization, 21
University of Alabama, 24, 69,
100, 101
University of Mississippi, 24, 90,
91
urban planning, 18–19

vagrancy, 14–15
Vietnam War, 28, 29
violence

cannot achieve racial justice, 113–14
development of tolerance for, 148
fear of, 116, 154
has political value, 142–43, 145
is immoral, 111, 113–14
is response
  of desegregation, 76–77
  only if outcome is not determined, 187–88
  of segregation, 39–40
led to Civil Rights Act, 145
in North, 164
  busing and, 161, 184, 185–88
  by protesters, 141
against police, 185
by police
  in Albany, 96–97
  in Birmingham, 25
  Supreme Court and, 96
  in Tallahassee, 140
  use of dogs, 145
relies on hatred, 111
retaliatory
  is strategy of nonviolent resistance, 109, 141, 142–45, 148–49
  value of, 145–46, 147–48
in South
  Freedom Rides and, 25, 122, 124, 125
  sit-ins and, 134, 139, 140

social system and, 32
voting. *See* suffrage

Wallace, George C.
  inaugural address of, 75–80
  segregation pledge of, 100
  University of Alabama and, 24
Warren, Earl, 61, 63, 64
Washington, Booker T., 20
Washington, D.C., 23
Washington, George, 80
Watts Manufacturing Company, 177
Western Springs, Illinois, 167
White, Kevin H., 185, 187, 188
white flight, 19
white liberalism, 174–76
white supremacy
  described, 33
  is unifying principle of South, 61, 63, 76
  segregation and, 12
  Southerners know truth of, 53, 59–60
Whittaker, Charles E., 64
Wilson, Clarence, 164, 167
Woolworth's, 137–38, 139
World War II, 21–22

Young, Andrew, 148
Yvon, Jean-Louis André, 186

Zinn, Howard, 90